APPLE

Dedicated to my inspirations in both food and life:
my grandmothers, Nanno and Nanny.

APPLE

James Rich

RECIPES FROM THE ORCHARD

Hardie Grant

BOOKS

An Apple a Day

'An apple a day, keeps the doctor away' or so goes the old English proverb. Actually, I think that our love affair with the apple runs far deeper and further than just that of something to nourish us and help keep us healthy – although I admit they do pack a punch when it comes to vitamins A and C, magnesium and fibre. While it's true that the apple does put a spring in our step, I think it plays, and has played, a big part in our lives for many other reasons too.

Apples and humans have a long and illustrious past. Grown, harvested and eaten for centuries, they have been a constant not only in our kitchens, but also as symbols within our culture, history, science and even modern technology, as well as featuring in religious texts and myths. From Newton's apple epiphany to apples being referenced as the fruit hanging from the tree of life that Heracles sought out in Greek mythology, they've long held symbolic power. Of course, they also famously feature in the *Book of Genesis*, referring to the forbidden fruit in the garden of Eden, though this is hotly disputed (especially as the fig leaf is the only reference made to any trees).

You might say that the apple is a beacon of human health and prosperity, and very few other fruits, or even vegetables for that matter, have had as big an impact or been as symbolic as that of the humble but unapologetic apple. In fact, you might even say that the apple is so important, so intrinsically entwined with human history and everyday life, that it deserves its very own book: a celebration of one of the most important and popular fruits in the world.

While I know this isn't the first, and certainly won't be the last, book written on the subject of the apple, this is my celebration. The recipes I've collected here feature the apple as their hero in all its forms – from whole apples to apple compôte, and cider to cider brandy – almost 100 recipes featuring all kinds of varieties. You'll find traditional old favourites, like apple crumble and pork with cider, as well as some new experiments and flavour combinations from my kitchen. A personal fanfare to the absolutely not-so-forbidden fruit.

My Family

My personal connection to apples started at a very young age, having grown up in the countryside of Somerset, in south-west England, which is full of apple orchards and the home of English cider. Some of my fondest memories are of exploring verdant apple orchards with my sisters; climbing trees and rummaging through the thickets to find creatures like frogs, toads and newts sheltering under old pieces of wood and in ponds and ditches. All the while, dad tended to, and pruned the apple trees.

My father is a master cider maker and, along with our cousins, continues the family business that has been producing traditional Somerset cider for generations. In fact, we're not quite sure how far back the cider-making goes in my family, but there are records of the Rich family in the area since 1612.

Much of Somerset is below sea level, known as the Somerset levels. In centuries past, this resulted in a scarcity of safe drinking water. Because of the lack of any water drainage or filtration systems the water that was available could carry all sorts of nasties that frequently made people ill and even caused fatalities.

It was logical, then, that the people resorted to drinking other forms of liquid to ensure they got their daily hydration. Landowners and farmers would make cider, which through the fermenting process killed any harmful bacteria, and would often trade cider as payment or part-payment in return for labour. The farmers and landowners got their hard physical jobs completed and the workers got their safe 'drinking water'. This barter of labour for one of the essentials of life went on for centuries before modern water services were installed, and it is generally accepted as part of the reason that cider, and also beer, came to prominence.

Cider-making officially became a family business when my great-uncle Gordon opened the gates to Mill Farm in 1954, selling Somerset's golden nectar to the public. Rich's Cider Farm grew from strength to strength as cider became increasingly popular, and is now run by Gordon's daughter, Jan, and her family along with my dad.

I have many memories of helping Dad out on the cider farm while growing up: planting the orchards, harvesting the apples, pressing them to gather the juice for making, and even clambering inside the giant 5,700-litre (10,000-pint) oak vats that are used during the fermenting process, to help clean them out.

Today, the cider farm not only encompasses the cider-making facilities, but it also has a shop, museum and restaurant. I may be biased, but what my family doesn't know about the famous apple, quite simply, isn't worth knowing.

All About Apples

There are more than 2,500 varieties of apple grown in the UK and more than 4,500 in the USA. Some have been cultivated for centuries – there is evidence, for example, in the Jordan Valley of apples dating back to 6,500 BC – while other types are relatively young. New varieties are being discovered and bred every year as global demand continues to grow.

*APPLE BLOSSOM

Apple blossom also has a role to play in keeping us healthy. Not only does it bear the buds that form into apples, but it is also very high in antioxidants and has been said to reduce stress and aid digestion. Apple blossom can be brewed as a tea, added to a cocktail or drink, or used as a garnish for salads and cakes. Flowering from April to June, apple blossom petals have a citrus-like flavour and the stems can taste similar to rhubarb.

The apple, or *Malus domestica*, is a member of the rose family. It is related closely not only to pears and quinces, but also plums, blackberries and even strawberries. It is widely accepted that apple trees originate from the forests of Kazakstan and that the Romans were largely responsible for the movement of trees around its Empire, creating popular demand for the fruit and cementing it as a mainstay of the diet throughout many regions of the world.

Everything from the apple blossom* to the fallen fruit can be used in cooking, making apples a hardy, versatile and delicious essential in the kitchen. Even smoking apple wood on the barbecue imparts a subtle sweet and fruity flavour to meat, fish and vegetables.

Apples come in many different shapes and sizes, flavours and textures. There are thousands of varieties across the world, each with distinctive characteristics that make it most suitable to be enjoyed in particular recipes.

Much of this depth of variety is thanks to the fact that every apple tree is unique. Most apple trees breed through cross-pollination: the pollen from one tree being deposited on the stigma of another tree – by bees and insects or by the wind – to fertilise it. Trees belong to specific, compatible pollinating groups that give the best resulting fruit. The seeds from each apple of that tree create independent offspring, because they are a cross between the original tree and the one that it has been pollinated with. The fruit of the resulting tree will therefore be a mix between the two parents and a different apple to the original parent or even its sibling trees. This can often result in orchards having a tendency to being home to a whole host of apple tree varieties and mixes growing together.

To help combat this and generate consistent apples from the trees, master apple growers cultivate their trees in a very specific way, by taking the rootstock, which is an existing and established set of roots, and grafting a tree bud or growth to that stock. This results in a tree that is healthy, and crucially that is a direct replica of the original tree, and therefore one that will bear the same fruit. (Pears, plums, cherries and medlars are also grown in this way.)

Using rootstock allows consumers to buy apples of a consistent style and variety from supermarkets or suppliers. While the more random style of natural pollination gives us the opportunity to buy unique local apples from farm shops or smaller outlets. That sounds like the best of both worlds!

Categories of Apples

Apples are generally categorised according to their tannin content – the natural preservative found in apple skin, seeds and stems – and acidity. They fall into one of four groups: sweet, sharp, bittersharp or bittersweet. Eating (dessert) apples generally fall somewhere between sweet and sharp. Sharp apples include a few eating apples and most cooking apples. Bittersharp and bittersweet are used to make cider.

Sweet apples have a higher sugar content, lower acid and lower tannins compared to the other apple categories, and therefore make ideal apples for eating raw. The vast majority of apples you will find in supermarkets the world over are sweet apples.

Popular sweet apple varieties
Gala, Golden Delicious, Braeburn, Fiji, Jazz and Honeycrisp.

Sharp apples have a higher acid count than sweet apples, but are low in tannin and sugar. They can require cooking to be edible, as with Bramley apples, but also include some eating apple varieties, and are widely used for apple juice.

Popular sharp apple varieties
Granny Smith, Cox's, Russet and Bramleys.

Bittersweet apples have a low level of sugar and acidity but a high level of tannin, while a *bittersharp* has high levels of both acidity and tannin, which make them perfect as the basis for cider-making. Bittersharp apples are the heroes of cider. Cider-making is all about blending and you can find different categories of apple – sharp and sweet as well as bittersweet – used in various ciders depending on what flavour the cider-maker is trying to achieve. Cider-making, like wine-making and beer-brewing, is both a science and an art.

Popular bittersweet and bittersharp apple varieties
Kingston Black, Lambrook Pippin, Yarlington, Dunkerton's Late, Chisel Jersey and Harry Master's.

1.

4.

2.

5.

3.

6.

Apple Varieties

While it would be impossible to create a definitive list of apples for the purposes of this book – there are so many that it would be an encyclopaedia in itself – I wanted to share a small selection of the most popular cooking and eating apple varieties that are widely available, some more common than others but each with their own distinctive flavour and story to tell.

1. ANNIE ELIZABETH

A particularly sweet cooking variety that works well in cakes as it keeps its shape, which make it ideal for decorating the tops of tarts and galettes.

2. BLENHEIM ORANGE

A dual-purpose variety that can be eaten as well as cooked. Great in dessert, crumbles and cakes.

3. BRAEBURN

Originally grown in New Zealand, this is a hardy and robust eating apple. Juicy, well balanced and with an interesting taste combination that includes a subtle hint of nutmeg and cinnamon flavours, Braeburns hold their shape when cooked and are great stuffed and baked.

4. BRAMLEYS

There is a reason why Bramleys are the undisputed king of the cookers: they have a durable, bitter sharp-flavour that mellows and sweetens when cooked. Bramleys are known the world over and easy to find in supermarkets. They also have a fascinating history, hailing from Southwell in Nottinghamshire UK, they were first recorded in 1809. The original tree that bore the very first Bramley apple fruit is still alive and producing apples each year, two centuries on.

5. CHIVERS DELIGHT

Not dissimilar to a Cox's, this has a good balance of sweet and sharp and a subtle aroma. It can be eaten raw or used in cooking.

6. COX'S

Arguably the most famous – and delicious, if you ask me – eating apple in the world, the Cox's Orange Pippin, to use its full title, is crisp, juicy and perfectly balanced. Intensely sweet but with a hefty level of sharp flavour, it can be eaten raw and used in cooking and baking too, where it keeps its shape well.

7. CRAB

Tiny green or blush-coloured apples that are about the size of a large cherry, crab apples have beautiful blossom and have recently been grown for their decorative properties rather than to be eaten, however they have an amazingly tangy flavour when cooked. Generally, they are too sharp to be eaten raw, unless picked at the end of the season, but they are great in pies and make perfect preserving apples for jams and jellies due to their very high pectin levels. pectin levels.

8. DISCOVERY

Originally from the county of Essex in the UK, Discovery apples are crisp and juicy with hints of strawberry in the flavour. Nicely balanced between sweet and sharp, they are ideal eaten raw in salads or juiced.

9. EGREMONT RUSSET

A very distinctive eating apple from the Russet family with golden-yellow, rough skin, Egremont Russet has a distinctive nutty and even smoky flavour, which makes them particularly delicious for juicing.

10. FIESTA

One of my favourite apples and similar in flavour and composition to the Cox's, which is actually its parent, Fiestas have a balanced sharp and sweet flavour, are aromatic and easily cooked, eaten raw or juiced. The skin is also the most wonderful deep red colour.

11. FUJI

Hailing from Japan with a crisp, juicy and sweet flavour, Fuji apples are generally best eaten raw, sliced into salads or used in drinks.

12. GOLDEN DELICIOUS

A very popular eating apple in the UK and Europe, Golden Delicious are crisp and juicy with a rich, sweet flavour when picked late in the season. An ideal eating apple, it needs to be used in simple, delicate dishes when cooked to avoid it being overshadowed by stronger, bolder flavours.

13. GRANNY SMITH

Intensely juicy, bold, sharp and packing a punch, Granny Smith is a hugely popular eating apple that also holds its own when cooked, in terms of both flavour and shape. Granny Smith can be cooked in many ways and is also great for juicing.

7.

11.

8.

12.

9.

13.

10.

14. HONEYCRISP

Crisp and sweet, a diverse eating apple that can be used across the board, from roasting to juicing. They are particularly good dried or made into apple crisps.

15. JAMES GRIEVE

A dual-purpose apple that is great when cooked in pastries and pies, but particularly when juiced, and you can also eat it raw, but you need to wait until later in the season when the fruit sweetens. A great alternative to Bramley.

16. JAZZ

A very young variety in apple terms, having been grown for the first time in New Zealand in the 1980s, Jazz apples are very juicy and crunchy with a sweet/tart balance and almost pear-like flavour. They can be used in pies, baking and are great in drinks too.

17. RED DELICIOUS

Mild, sweet and delicately flavoured, Red Delicious are a popular and widely available eating apple in the USA, in particular. Although similar to the Golden Delicious in its flavour, the two are not actually related. Good for eating, this isn't a great apple to cook with due to its delicate flavour.

18. RED FALSTAFF

Usually eaten fresh and great for juicing, this apple has an aromatic flavour and sweet-sharp balance.

19. ROYAL GALA

One of the most widely available apples on the planet, Royal Gala apples are crisp, juicy and sweet with floral and vanilla notes. Incredibly diverse, Royal Galas are great eating apples and can also be used in salads, chutneys and preserves, baking, and even diced into burger patties.

20. WORCESTER PEARMAIN

First noted in 1874, the Worcester Pearmain is a crisp, aromatic apple with unusual strawberry notes.

All the recipes give suggested varieties that should be readily available. However, if you are lucky enough to be able to search out local varieties, simply use the suggestions to pick an unusual variety that has similar qualities.

14.

15.

16.

17.

18.

19.

20.

The following notes apply to all recipes unless otherwise stated.

Do not mix metric and imperial measurements.

1 teaspoon = 5 ml, 1 tablespoon = 15 ml, 1 cup = 250 ml.

Use medium fruits and vegetables.

Use large, free-range eggs.

Use fresh ingredients, including herbs and spices.

Recipes suggest readily available apple varieties but you can substitute any other varieties with similar flavour and qualities.

Only peel apples if the recipe specifically calls for it.

Use apples as soon as possible after preparation as they will discolour if left open to the air. If that is not possible, toss the prepared apples in a little lemon juice.

All recipes use the British term for cider, scrumpy and apple juice. Cider and scrumpy are alcoholic and equivalent to the American 'hard cider'; apple juice is non-alcoholic and equivalent to the American 'cider'.

All ovens vary in their cooking temperatures so you need to get to know yours. If necessary, use an oven thermometer.

All recipes have been tested in a fan-assisted oven at the given temperatures, but these should be treated as a guide only. If you are cooking in a conventional, non-fan-assisted oven, you should increase the temperatures by 10–20°C (50–60°F).

Sterilising Jars

It is important to sterilise any jars you're using for the chutney, pickle or relish recipes to ensure they are perfectly clean, which will make sure your produce keeps nicely protected for as long as possible.

If you have a dishwasher, put the jars and lids through a cycle in the dishwasher. If not, follow this simple procedure.

1. Wash your jars and lids in hot soapy water and rinse thoroughly.

2. Pop the jars on a baking sheet in a preheated fan oven at 120°C (250°F/gas 1) for 20 minutes.

3. Put the metal lids – or the rubber seal that come with Kilner (Mason) jars – in a saucepan with boiling water and boil for 5 minutes.

4. Remove the jars from the oven and the lids or seals from the pan and let them cool until ready to handle. Fill with your chosen produce immediately, seal and label with the name and the date.

Light Bites

Apple flavours can be delicate and complementary,
floral and simple or they can be bold, sharp and
stand out from the crowd. This is a collection
of quick recipes, from breakfasts through to easy
lunches and light suppers, that let the apple flavour
sing. Crisp, nutty granola and cheese tarts, these
light bites have the joyful apple at the very core.

Nutty apple granola

Nutty apple granola makes a tasty, filling and nutritious breakfast, served on its own, with milk or with yoghurt, a dollop of Apple and vanilla compôte (page 126) and some Apple crisps (page 111). Once baked, this granola will last about a week in an airtight container. You can use your favourite mixture of nuts and seeds – brazil nuts, pecans, hazelnuts, almonds, pumpkin seeds and sunflower seeds are all delicious.

Serves 12
Prep 10 mins
Cook 30 mins

400 g (14 oz/4 cups) rolled
  jumbo oats
200 g (7 oz/2 cups)
  mixed nuts and seeds,
  roughly chopped
½ teaspoon ground cinnamon
¼ teaspoon ground ginger
¼ teaspoon freshly
  grated nutmeg
a few drops of vanilla extract
150 ml (5 fl oz/scant
  ⅔ cup) maple syrup
  or runny honey
1 sharp, green eating
  (dessert) apple, such as
  Granny Smith, cored and
  chopped into small chunks
75 g (2½ oz/⅔ cup) raisins

Preheat a fan oven to 160°C (320°F/gas 4) and line a large baking sheet with baking parchment.

Put the oats, nuts and seeds, cinnamon, ginger and nutmeg in a large mixing bowl and mix together well. In a separate bowl, add the vanilla extract to the maple syrup or honey, then stir it through the oat mixture until everything is coated. Add the apple chunks and mix through.

Turn out onto the prepared baking sheet and spread evenly. Bake in the oven for 15 minutes, stirring the granola halfway through.

Add the raisins to the granola and mix together. I do this to avoid the raisins overbaking as they have a tendency to burn a little. However, if you don't mind crunchy raisins, then feel free to add these with the rest of the ingredients.

Return to the oven and finish baking for a further 10–15 minutes, stirring halfway through, until crisp and golden.

Remove from the oven and leave to cool fully before decanting into a large airtight container. It will keep for up to a week in an airtight container, but it is moister than other granolas so keep an eye on it.

Apple and banana bircher

This is the perfect, no-hassle yet delicious and healthy breakfast that can be prepared overnight ready to grab and go. I love this made with coconut yoghurt but you can easily swap for your favourite alternative, and top with Nutty apple granola (page 38) and either the Apple and vanilla compôte (page 126) or the Crab apple and blackberry jam (page 119).

Serves 2
Prep 10 mins +
  overnight chilling

1 sharp, green eating
  (dessert) apple, such
  as Granny Smith, cored
  and grated (shredded)
50 g (2 oz/¼ cup) rolled oats
50 g (2 oz/heaped ⅓ cup)
  mixed seeds and nuts,
  toasted (hazelnuts,
  Brazil nuts, sunflower
  seeds and pecans is my
  favourite combination)
100 g (3½ oz/scant ½ cup)
  coconut yoghurt
20 g (¾ oz) raspberries
20 g (¾ oz/scant ¼ cup)
  sultanas (golden raisins)
1 banana

Mix the apple, oats and half the seed and nut mix into the coconut yoghurt and refrigerate overnight.

Take the yoghurt and apple mix out of the refrigerator, stir in the raspberries and divide into two bowls or jam jars. Top with the sultanas and the rest of the nuts and seeds, slice the banana over the top and you're ready to go!

Barszcz

Barszcz – which is the Polish name for what is more familiarly known as the Russian name of *borscht* – can be a messy business! The beetroot can get absolutely everywhere and stains most things, so rubber gloves and an apron are highly recommended when preparing this deeply flavoursome dish. Traditionally borscht hails from Eastern Europe and is a hearty staple across the region. The earthy beetroot flavour mixed with the stock, vegetables and sweet/sharp apple is like a big warming hug from home, ideal for lunches on cold winter days and an essential if you're feeling under the weather. This version uses chicken stock, but if you want to make it vegetarian or vegan, then swap for a good vegetable stock and omit the sour cream.

Serves 4
Prep 15 mins
Cook 35 mins

2 tablespoons olive oil
1 large onion, chopped
2 garlic cloves, finely chopped
1 large potato, peeled and
   finely diced
1 celery stalk, finely chopped
1 large carrot, finely diced
4 large raw beetroot,
   2 peeled and cubed, 2 peeled
   and grated (shredded)
½ teaspoon allspice
1 large cooking apple, such
   as Bramley, peeled, cored
   and cubed
¼ white cabbage, cored
   and shredded
400 g (14 oz) tin of red kidney
   beans, rinsed and drained
3 tablespoons tomato ketchup
2 bay leaves
juice of ½ lemon
1.5 litres (56 fl oz/6⅔ cups)
   chicken stock
salt and freshly ground
   black pepper

To serve
1 tablespoon dill leaves
2 tablespoons sour cream
crusty bread

In a large saucepan, heat the oil over a medium heat, add the onion and fry for a couple minutes until it starts to soften. Add the garlic, potato, celery, carrot and cubed beetroot and fry for a further 5 minutes.

Stir in the allspice and cook for 2 minutes.

Add the grated beetroot, apple, cabbage and beans and stir in well. Fry with the other vegetables for 2 minutes, then stir in the tomato ketchup, bay leaves and lemon juice.

Finally, add the chicken stock, bring everything to the boil and season with salt and pepper. Reduce to a simmer for about 20 minutes until the vegetables are cooked, but retain some firmness.

Sprinkle with a few dill leaves and serve in bowls with a dollop of sour cream and some chunks of crusty bread.

Apple, turmeric and fennel soup

There's nothing better on a cool autumn evening than a warming bowl of spicy soup. Apples are great in soups, especially Bramleys. They break down adding a base note of sweetness while enhancing the other flavours in the dish. I love this recipe; in my mind it's the perfect balance of savoury, sweet and spicy. If you want to take the heat up a notch, you can add more chilli (hot pepper) flakes at the end, but don't go over the top with the turmeric. It's a bold and confident flavour that can easily overpower, but used correctly will provide a golden warmth.

Serves 4
Prep 20 mins
Cook 45 mins

2 tablespoons extra
   virgin olive oil, plus extra
   for serving
2 leeks, trimmed and chopped
1 onion, chopped
1 fennel bulb, roughly
   chopped, reserving
   any leaves to garnish
2 cooking apples, such
   as Bramleys, cored and
   chopped (about 350 g/12 oz)
2 sprigs of thyme
2 teaspoons ground turmeric
750 ml (25 fl oz/3 cups)
   vegetable stock
salt and freshly ground
   black pepper
handful of walnuts, very
   roughly chopped
drizzle of Apple syrup
   (page 116) or runny honey

To serve
chilli (hot pepper) flakes
fennel leaves

Heat the olive oil in a large heavy-based saucepan over a medium heat. Add the leeks, onion and fennel and fry for 5–7 minutes until everything starts to become translucent but without allowing it to brown. Keep an eye on the mixture as you don't want anything to burn or stick at all.

Add the apples and thyme and fry for a further 2–3 minutes to allow the apples to start to cook.

Then add the turmeric and give everything a good stir to coat all the ingredients in the pan equally. Fry for another 3 minutes, stirring occasionally. The fruit and vegetables will start to stick and go slightly brown – that's okay at this point, but you don't want them to burn.

Add the vegetable stock and season with salt and pepper. Bring the pan to the boil for a minute and then reduce to a simmer for 30 minutes. The fruit and vegetables need to be nice and soft and thoroughly cooked. You might need a little more or less time here, so keep watch.

While the soup is cooking, heat a non-stick frying pan (skillet) over a medium heat and toast the walnuts for a couple minutes, ensuring they don't burn.

Add a little apple syrup or honey to the nuts, shaking the pan, until it begins to bubble and the walnuts are thoroughly coated. Turn the walnuts out onto a plate lined with baking parchment and leave to one side to cool.

Once the soup is cooked, leave to cool slightly before whizzing in a food processor in batches or blitz with a hand-held blender in the pan. You need to get it really smooth. If it's too thick, add a little water or more stock.

Serve by filling bowls with soup and topping with the caramelised walnuts, a sprinkle of chilli flakes, some fennel leaves and a drizzle of olive oil – or any combination you like.

Black pudding and caramelised apple

The flavours of black pudding and apple remind me of home. My grandmother has cooked me this for breakfast ever since I was small, but you can equally serve it as part of a warm winter salad or starter. The deep, earthy flavour of black pudding and sweet, warm apple complement each other perfectly.

Serves 4
Prep 5 mins
Cook 4–6 mins

50 g (2 oz) butter
2 crisp, red eating (dessert)
  apples, such as Braeburn
200 g (7 oz) black pudding,
  skinned and sliced
salt and freshly ground
  black pepper

To serve
thick buttered toast

Heat the butter in a frying pan (skillet) over a medium heat. Core and slice the apples into 8 wedges, then add them to the pan. Fry for 2 minutes until the apples begin to soften.

Add the black pudding to the pan and fry for 1–2 minutes on each side until it begins to go crispy and crunchy on the outside, being careful not to overcook.

Season with a little salt and pepper and serve with some thick, buttered toast.

Curried parsnip and apple soup

I am a big fan of parsnips and their subtle herby sweetness, which incidentally makes them a great companion to apples. Throw in some curry spices and you have an aromatic and flavourful bowl of hearty warmth. This soup is very quick and easy to make – and what's more will fill your home with beautiful sweet and spicy aromas while it cooks.

Serves 4
Prep 15 mins
Cook 35 mins

2 tablespoons olive oil
1 onion, chopped
600 g (1 lb 5 oz) parsnips,
   peeled and chopped
2 medium potatoes, peeled
   and chopped
2 garlic cloves, crushed
1½ teaspoons curry powder
1½ teaspoons ground coriander
1 teaspoon ground ginger
salt and freshly ground
   black pepper
1 cooking apple, such
   as a Bramley, peeled,
   cored and chopped
1 litre (34 fl oz/4 cups)
   chicken stock
juice of ½ lemon

To serve
crème fraîche
coriander seeds, toasted
   and crushed

Heat the olive oil in a large saucepan over a medium heat. Add the onion and fry for 2 minutes. Then add the parsnips and potatoes and fry for a further 5 minutes until they begin to soften. Add the garlic and fry for a further 2 minutes.

Throw in the spices and some salt and pepper and give everything a good stir with a wooden spoon to allow the spices to toast. Add the apple and fry for 1 minute.

Add the chicken stock and bring to the boil. Reduce to a simmer and cook for 25 minutes until all the vegetables are soft and mush easily with the wooden spoon. Take off the heat and leave to cool.

Blitz the soup in batches using a food processor or hand-held blender until it is smooth. When everything is blended, add the lemon juice and stir.

To serve, warm the soup, then ladle into bowls. Top with a swirl of crème fraîche and a sprinkling of crushed, toasted coriander seeds.

Fiery apple and walnut rice salad

I started experimenting with a rice salad because my sister, Beck, makes a delicious hearty bowl of it at every family get together we have, but refused to share her secret recipe with me for this book. This wasn't a surprise, we have a 'healthy' competitive relationship, and there was absolutely no prising the recipe from her vice-like grip.

Her rice salad is always so popular that I just had to include one, so it was up to me to create my own. She adds apple to hers, and walnuts, some spices and spring onions, but that is pretty much where the comparisons end. What I've ended up with is something quite different, but equally as tasty – even if I do say so myself!

Serves 4
Prep 15 mins
Cook 30 mins

250 g (9 oz/1¼ cups) black
  rice, washed
1 teaspoon salt
2 little gem (bibb) lettuces
1 teaspoon olive oil
½ teaspoon ground cumin
2 crisp, sweet eating (dessert)
  apples, such as Cox's or
  Fiesta, cored and chopped
2 carrots, peeled and
  grated (shredded)
4 spring onions
  (scallions), chopped
50 g (2 oz/½ cup) walnuts,
  roughly chopped and toasted
small bunch of coriander
  (cilantro) leaves, chopped

For the dressing
zest and juice of 2 limes
4 teaspoons runny honey
2 red bird's eye chillies,
  finely chopped
4 tablespoons olive oil
2 tablespoons shop-bought
  or homemade Apple cider
  vinegar (page 133)
salt and freshly ground
  black pepper

Put the black rice and salt in a saucepan, cover with plenty of water, bring to the boil, then simmer until just tender. This will usually take about 30 minutes. Drain well.

Meanwhile, wash the lettuce leaves and place in a large serving bowl.

Heat the oil in a frying pan (skillet) for 1–2 minutes over a low heat until hot. Add the ground cumin and fry gently for 1 minute. Add the rice to the pan and mix well. Stir for a further couple of minutes before taking off the heat and leaving to cool.

Meanwhile, put the dressing ingredients in a bowl and mix well.

When the rice has cooled, stir in the apples, grated carrots, spring onions and walnuts, then spoon the rice on top of the lettuce. Drizzle with the dressing and fork through to mix. Garnish with the coriander leaves, to serve.

Avocado and apple salad

I like to think this salad is a celebration of wonder-foods young and old. The past few years has seen the avocado hailed and celebrated for its fatty, nutritious goodness. The apple, however, has arguably been celebrated in a similar way for much, much longer. I like to think of the apple as the original superfood.

Serves 4
Prep 15 mins
Cook 30 mins

2 crisp eating (dessert)
  apples, such as Cox's
  or Fiesta
squeeze of lemon juice
75 g (3 oz/¾ cup) walnuts,
  roughly chopped
1 tablespoon Apple syrup
  (page 116) or runny honey
1 head of chicory (endive),
  cored and leaves separated
75 g (3 oz) watercress
2 ripe avocados, peeled,
  pitted and thickly sliced
75 g (3 oz) feta

For the dressing
4 tablespoons olive oil
1 garlic clove, crushed
1 cm (½ in) piece of ginger root,
  peeled and grated (shredded)
1 tablespoon shop-bought
  or homemade Apple cider
  vinegar (page 133)
1 tablespoon runny honey
1 tablespoon light soy sauce

Line a plate with baking parchment. Core and thickly slice the apple and place in a bowl of water with the lemon juice. This will stop it from browning and keep it fresh.

Heat a small frying pan (skillet) over a medium-high heat, add the walnuts and toast in the pan for 2 minutes, tossing regularly so they do not burn. Then add the apple syrup or honey and mix with the nuts. Heat for no more than 30 seconds until the syrup bubbles around the nuts, then pour onto the prepared plate and leave to cool and harden. Once cooled, roughly chop or crumble.

To make the dressing, whisk together all the ingredients until well combined. Set aside.

In a large salad bowl, place the chicory leaves, watercress and half the avocado. Drain the apples and add half to the bowl. Mix in half the dressing to coat the salad leaves, avocado and apple evenly.

Top with the rest of the apple and avocado, crumble over the feta and candied walnuts. Finally, drizzle over the remaining dressing to serve.

Classic Waldorf salad

The combination of apple, grapes, walnuts, crisp lettuce and mayonnaise is a firm favourite go-to summer salad. The flavours – the sweet juice of the apple, nutty, woody walnut tones and the freshness of the lettuce – just work together like a dream. There's really nothing that can begin to improve on this classic combination, so I was originally going to leave this one out. However, when talking to my friends and family about the recipes that would form this collection of apple celebrations, the Waldorf came up time and time again.

It may be a little retro, but that in itself is something to celebrate as far as I'm concerned. In my opinion, the best apples to use here are sharp, yet sweet Cox's, and if you do want take this dish to the next level, then add some grilled (broiled) chicken or prawns (shrimps) to turn this into a hearty meal.

Serves 4
Prep 20 mins
Cook 15 mins

50 g (2 oz) seedless grapes
juice of ½ lemon
50 g (2 oz/½ cup) walnut halves
6 tablespoons mayonnaise
½ teaspoon Dijon mustard
salt and freshly ground
  black pepper
2 little gem (bibb) lettuces,
  roughly chopped
2 sweet, juicy eating (dessert)
  apples, such as Cox's, cored
  and chopped
2 celery stalks, sliced

Preheat a fan oven to 160°C (320°F/gas 4).

Place the grapes on a baking sheet and squeeze over the lemon juice. Bake in the oven for 10 minutes until they start to shrink.

Add the walnuts and cook for a further 5 minutes until toasted. Leave to one side to cool.

Next, mix the mayonnaise and mustard together in a bowl with a pinch of salt and some pepper.

In a serving bowl, add the lettuce leaves, apple slices and celery. When the walnuts are cool add them and the grapes to the bowl.

Add the mustard-mayo and mix thoroughly to combine then serve.

Crunchy apple, cherry and kale salad

This salad is deliciously different. The flavours and juiciness of the cherries and apple complement the dark green richness of the kale and cabbage like a marriage made in salad-y heaven. Plus, the addition of the syrup-coated nuts gives it a hearty crunch for something truly unique. I've played about with the stone fruit combination and apricots, peaches and grapes work well here too.

Serves 4
Prep 10 mins
Cook 5 mins

50 g (2 oz/⅓ cup) almonds, very roughly chopped
50 g (2 oz/½ cup) pecans, very roughly chopped
2 tablespoons Apple syrup (page 116) or runny honey
400 g (14 oz) kale
200 g (7 oz) green cabbage
2 tablespoons mayonnaise
100 g (3½ oz/scant ½ cup) natural yoghurt
1 sprig of fresh rosemary leaves, finely chopped
1 teaspoon shop-bought or homemade Apple cider vinegar (page 133)
2 sharp, green eating (dessert) apples, such as Granny Smith
50 g (2 oz) fresh cherries, pitted and halved

Line a plate with baking parchment. Heat a small frying pan (skillet) over a medium-high heat and toast the nuts in the pan for 2–3 minutes, tossing regularly so they do not burn. Then quickly add the apple syrup or honey and mix with the nuts. Heat for no more than 30 seconds until the syrup bubbles around the nuts, before pouring everything out onto the baking parchment-lined plate and leaving to cool and harden. Once cooled, roughly chop or crumble.

Wash the kale and cabbage and chop into 2.5 cm (1 in) pieces, discarding the woody and tough centres. Dry using paper towels and put one side.

In a large mixing bowl, mix the mayo, yoghurt, rosemary and vinegar, then add the cabbage and kale and combine thoroughly.

Core and slice the apple, leaving the skin on, and add to the bowl with the cherries. Mix well.

Finally, top the salad with the toasted nuts and serve.

Cauliflower, pomegranate and apple salad

This salad makes a delicious mid-summer meal. While I've housed it here in the Light Bites section and written the recipe to serve four, you could easily make this as a main meal for two. The crisp apple and pomegranate seeds bring a lip-puckering tartness to the cauliflower, nuts and spices.

Serves 4
Prep 20 mins
Cook 25 mins

1 cauliflower, trimmed
   and cut into florets
2 tablespoons olive oil
½ teaspoon paprika
½ teaspoon ground cumin
50 g (2 oz/½ cup) skin-on
   almonds, roughly chopped
2 sharp, green eating
   (dessert) apples, such
   as Granny Smith
squeeze of lemon juice
1 pomegranate, seeds only
150 g (5 oz) wild rocket
   (arugula) leaves

For the dressing
1 tablespoon tahini
1 tablespoon runny honey
1 tablespoon lemon juice
1 tablespoon olive oil
salt and freshly ground
   black pepper

Preheat a fan oven to 160°C (320°C/gas 4) and line a medium baking sheet with baking parchment.

Put the cauliflower florets, olive oil, paprika, cumin and almonds in a large bowl and mix well, making sure the cauliflower is evenly coated with the oil and spices. Tip out onto the baking sheet and roast in the oven for 25 minutes until the cauliflower has started to brown. Take out of the oven and leave to cool.

Meanwhile, core and chop the apples into 1 cm (½ in) chunks and add to a bowl of cold water with the lemon juice – this will prevent them from browning and keep them nice and fresh.

Make the dressing by combining the tahini, honey, lemon juice and olive oil. Season with some salt and pepper.

Finally, drain the apples and combine with the cauliflower mix, pomegranate seeds and rocket, then drizzle over the dressing and serve.

Apple fritters

These fritters come with a warning: they are seriously addictive and utterly moreish, especially when eaten fresh and warm with a coffee. I also like them with a drizzle of icing sugar or a sprinkle of cinnamon sugar, so have included both options here. If I were you, I'd make both!

Makes 10
Prep 10 mins
Cook 15 mins

25 g (1 oz) butter
2 sharp, green eating
  (dessert) apples, such
  as Granny Smith, peeled,
  cored and cubed
300 g (10½ oz/2½ cups)
  plain (all-purpose) flour
50 g (2 oz/scant ¼ cup) caster
  (superfine) sugar
1 teaspoon baking powder
pinch of salt
¼ teaspoon ground cinnamon
¼ teaspoon ground ginger
pinch of freshly grated nutmeg
1 egg, beaten
90 ml (3 fl oz/⅓ cup)
  whole milk
½ vanilla pod (bean), cut
  in half lengthways and
  seeds scraped out
vegetable oil, for deep frying

For the cinnamon sugar coating
½ teaspoon ground cinnamon
50 g (2 oz/scant ¼ cup) caster
  (superfine) sugar

For the icing sugar coating
50 g (2 oz/scant ½ cup) icing
  (confectioner's) sugar

Heat the butter in a frying pan (skillet) over a medium heat until melted. Add the apple cubes and fry for 2–3 minutes until they begin to caramelise. Remove the apples using a slotted spoon and place them on some paper towel to soak up excess liquid.

In a large mixing bowl, sift together the flour, sugar, baking powder, salt, cinnamon, ginger and nutmeg.

In a separate bowl, whisk together the egg and milk, then add the apple cubes and the vanilla seeds. Mix well.

Gradually add the milk mixture to the flour mixture a little at a time, folding it in with a wooden spoon to form a batter.

When you're ready to cook the fritters, heat enough oil in a deep frying pan (skillet) to fill the pan to about 4 cm (1½ in) deep until very hot – 175°C (350°F). Test the heat by adding a small amount of batter to the oil. If it bubbles instantly and browns, then you're ready to go.

Cook the fritters in batches of about six at a time. Use two tablespoons to shape the batter into quenelles and carefully lower them into the hot oil to bubble away. Cook for 2–3 minutes or until they are golden brown. Using a slotted spoon, transfer the cooked fritters onto a plate lined with paper towels to dry. Then transfer to a wire rack.

If you are making cinnamon-sugar-coated fritters, combine the ground cinnamon and caster sugar and mix well. Roll the warm fritters in the cinnamon sugar while they are still hot.

If you are making icing-sugar fritters, wait until the fritters have fully cooled. Mix the icing sugar with a couple drops of water until you have a thick, smooth icing. Using a fork, drizzle the icing over the fritters and allow to set.

Apple, Cheddar and caramelised onion tart

Cheddar originates from Somerset – in fact I went to school in Cheddar itself – and there is nothing that Somerset-folk love more than apples, Cheddar, some onion and crusty bread, especially when washed down with a pint of scrumpy! The ideal Somerset lunch. This tart celebrates those splendid local flavours in a somewhat different way and makes a delicious light lunch or starter at dinner.

Serves 4
Prep 15 mins
Cook 25–35 mins

2 x 320 g (10¾ oz) sheets
   of ready-made puff pastry
a little plain (all-purpose)
   flour, for dusting
10 g (¼ oz) butter
1 large onion, thinly sliced
1 tablespoon dried thyme
freshly ground black pepper
150 g (5 oz) Cheddar
2 crisp, red eating (dessert)
   apples, such as Gala or Fiesta,
   cored and thinly sliced
25 g (1 oz/scant ¼ cup)
   pine nuts
1 egg, beaten

To serve
side salad (optional)

Preheat a fan oven to 200°C (400°F/gas 8) and line a baking sheet with baking parchment.

Roll out one of the pastry sheets on a lightly floured surface to about 30 x 45 cm (12 x 18 in), transfer to the prepared baking sheet and prick the sheet all over with a fork. Then roll the second sheet to the same size, but this time cut a smaller rectangle out of the pastry to form a frame-like piece that is about 1 cm (½ in) wide. Take out the inner rectangle and reserve for another recipe. Moisten the edges and place the frame over the first piece of pastry. This will form the puffed sides of the tart.

Next, melt the butter in a frying pan (skillet) and add the onion, thyme and a pinch of ground black pepper. Cook for 5 minutes to allow the onion to sweat and begin to brown.

Spread the onion and thyme mixture over the pastry base, within the frame, then grate the Cheddar evenly on top of the onion – the bigger the chunks of cheese, the better.

Now arrange the sliced apple on top, creating either fan decorations or rows of overlapping apple pieces. Lightly toast the pine nuts in a pan, then sprinkle over the pine nuts and a pinch more dried thyme.

Finally, brush the pastry edges with the beaten egg. Bake in the oven for 20–30 minutes until the pastry is nicely golden and crispy and the apples cooked and melting into the cheese. Serve either warm or cold as a side dish or starter, with or without a fresh salad.

Goat's cheese, apple and honey tarts

It's best to use a sweet apple for this recipe to complement the tanginess of the cheese, so try a Braeburn or Royal Gala instead of Granny Smith or Cox's. You can either bake this as individual tarts – as I have done – or as a traybake, in which case just roll out the puff pastry into a rectangle.

Makes 10
Prep 25 mins
Cook 30–40 mins

75 g (2½ oz) unsalted butter
1 onion, thinly sliced
½ sprig of rosemary, leaves
   removed and finely chopped
2 x 320 g (10¼ oz) packs
   of ready-made puff-pastry
a little plain (all-purpose)
   flour, for dusting
1 egg, beaten

For the cheese topping
200 g (7 oz) goat's cheese
1 tablespoon lemon juice
salt and freshly ground
   black pepper
4 crisp eating (dessert)
   apples, such as Braeburn,
   peeled, cored and sliced
pinch of ground allspice
4 tablespoons runny honey
micro purple basil

Preheat a fan oven to 180°C (350°F/gas 6) and line a large baking sheet with baking parchment.

Heat a saucepan over a medium heat and melt half the butter. Add the onion and rosemary and fry until the onion begins to brown. Leave to one side.

Roll out the pastry on a lightly floured surface to about 5 mm (¼ in) thick. Using a round, 10 cm (4 in) biscuit (cookie) cutter, cut out 20 rounds. Place 10 on the prepared baking sheet and prick all over with a fork.

Make pastry rings by cutting smaller rounds into the remaining 10 pieces of pastry using a 9 cm (3½ in) biscuit cutter. Then, take out the centre sections and save for another recipe. Brush the whole rounds on the baking sheet with the beaten egg, and then place a pastry ring on each one. Pop in the freezer for 15 minutes to cool.

To make the cheese topping, put the goat's cheese, lemon juice and some salt and pepper into a bowl and mix with a fork. Avoid over-mixing as you want the cheese to still be crumbly.

Spoon about 1 tablespoon of the cheese mix onto each piece of pastry, then top with the sliced apple, overlapping slightly.

Melt the remaining butter and brush it over the tarts. Sprinkle over the allspice.

Bake in the oven for 25–30 minutes until golden brown. When the tarts are out of the oven, drizzle with the honey and micro purple basil while still warm and serve.

Feasts

Soaked in cider, cooked slow and steady – that's pretty much the theme for an apple and cider feast, whether you're roasting a duck bathed in cider brandy, serving pork chops with apples or sharing spreads that include apple and coconut curry. Feasts are a time when apples really come into their own. In many savoury dishes, apples, cider and apple juice provide an added depth and enhanced flavour. This is a selection of recipes for those occasions when time isn't an issue and you want to really indulge in a meal worth celebrating.

Mussels in cider

The best part of eating mussels is, arguably, greedily mopping up those delicious cooking liquids and juices with chunks of bread and glistening fingers. The cider here is salty, sweet and smoky as it takes on the flavours of the mussels and smoked bacon – and is utterly moreish.

Serves 4
Prep 30 mins
Cook 15 mins

1.5 kg (3 lb 5 oz) mussels, cleaned
50 g (2 oz) unsalted butter
150 g (5 oz) smoked bacon
   pieces or about 8 slices
small bunch of thyme, leaves
   removed and chopped
300 ml (10 fl oz/1¼ cups)
   dry cider
3 spring onions
   (scallions), chopped

To serve
flat-leaf parsley
crusty bread
butter
lemon wedges

You can buy clean mussels in supermarkets or ask the fishmonger to do this for you, but it's not difficult if you need to do it yourself. Scrub the mussels and rinse in several changes of water. Scrape off any debris and pull or cut off the beards. If any mussels are open, tap them and they should shut. If they don't, discard them.

Heat the butter in a large, heavy-based pan with a good solid lid over a medium heat. Once it has melted, add the bacon and thyme and fry for a few minutes until the bacon is crisping up.

Turn the heat up to high, add the mussels and pour in the cider. Put the lid on and give the pan a good shake. Leave to steam for 5–8 minutes until all the mussels have opened. Throw away any that remain closed. Sprinkle over the spring onions and give everything a good stir.

Serve in a large bowl and garnish with some flat-leaf parsley. Place in the centre of the table, so that everybody can dig in, alongside some crusty bread and butter and some lemon wedges.

Apple, coconut and ginger curry

Apples and curry do not sound like they should form a dish together at all. But fruit works wonderfully in curries. In fact, I think they could be my favourite kind. Here, the tartness of the apples, combined with the flavours of chillies and spices, are soothed by coconut milk and together it forms something quite special. The dish can be eaten as a side or as it comes, alongside some rice or naan bread.

I really wanted to explore adding apples to curry and so the inspiration for this dish comes from a Caribbean recipe and another from Sri Lanka, a mix of East meets West. It's important to use sharp apples, such as Granny Smith, that will keep their shape when cooked. It's also important to leave the skin on. If you are looking for a milder version, then remove the seeds from one or both of the chillies. However, personally, I would go for full heat and add more coconut milk if it needs taming at all.

Serves 4
Prep 10 mins
Cook 25–35 mins

3 tablespoons vegetable oil
1 onion, finely chopped
1 tablespoon curry powder
½ teaspoon ground turmeric
1 teaspoon mustard seeds
½ teaspoon caraway seeds
4 dried red chillies, chopped
4 curry leaves
1 green bird's eye chilli, chopped
4 large sharp, green eating
    (dessert) apples, such
    as Granny Smith, quartered
    and cored
2 garlic cloves, finely chopped
2.5 cm (1 in) piece of ginger
    root, peeled and grated
    (shredded)
50 ml (1¾ fl oz/
    3 tablespoons) apple juice
400 g (14 oz) tin
    of coconut milk
salt and freshly ground
    black pepper

Heat half the oil in a large frying pan (skillet). Add the onion and fry for 3–4 minutes to soften. Next, add the curry powder, turmeric, mustard and caraway seeds and dried chillies and toast the spices for 1–2 minutes until fragrant.

Add the curry leaves, chopped chilli, apple quarters, garlic and ginger to the pan and stir well to mix everything together. Cook for 10–15 minutes to allow the apples to start to cook and soften.

Add the apple juice and simmer for a minute, then pour in the coconut milk and reduce to a slight simmer. Add salt to season and cook gently for 10 minutes until everything is well blended and the sauce is thick with the softened apple chunks.

Once the curry has cooked, season to taste with salt and pepper and serve with either some steamed rice or a chapati or naan bread.

Trout baked in cider

Trout is a delicious fish and one that I don't cook often enough. I wanted to see how well its flavour could work with cider. The good news is they work well, very well indeed. The gravy – or 'stock' is probably a more accurate description – is utterly delicious so please don't throw it away. Serve the stock with the fish and some vegetables or mashed potato. If you're struggling to find trout for this one, it can easily be swapped for mackerel.

Serves 4 (depending on the
   size of the trout)
Prep 10 mins
Cook 35 mins

1 fennel bulb, sliced
2 leeks, trimmed and sliced
100 g (3½ oz) frozen peas
2 large whole rainbow trout,
   scaled and gutted (ask your
   fishmonger to do this)
salt and freshly ground
   black pepper
1 lemon, sliced
1 soft, red eating (dessert)
   apple, such as Braeburn or
   Red Falstaff, cored and sliced
500 ml (17 fl oz/2 cups)
   dry cider
20 g (¾ oz) chervil or flat-leaf
   parsley leaves or 1 teaspoon
   dried chervil

Preheat a fan oven to 200°C (400°F/gas 8).

In a large ovenproof dish, layer the sliced fennel and leeks on the bottom, then pour the peas over the top.

Open up the trout and season with salt and pepper. Put the sliced lemon and apple in the trout belly, overlapping one slice of apple with one slice of lemon. Then place the trout on top of the vegetables.

Pour the cider over the fish and sprinkle with half the chervil or parsley (reserving the rest for garnish). Season with salt and pepper, cover and bake in the oven for 35 minutes until both fish and vegetables are nicely cooked.

Sprinkle with the chervil and serve.

Chicken, apricot and cider with miso

Miso is great with chicken and the flavours of the apricots take on a syrupy jamminess, mingling with the cider to create a sticky-sweet sensation. It is something a little different but, trust me, it is incredibly flavourful.

Serves 4
Prep 10 mins
Cook 40 mins

2 tablespoons olive oil
8 skin-on bone-in
  chicken thighs
1 onion, cut into wedges
4 large, ripe, fresh apricots,
  halved and pitted
2 tablespoons miso paste
500 ml (17 fl oz/2 cups)
  dry cider

To serve
1 tablespoon pine nuts
handful of parsley,
  roughly chopped
your choice of vegetables
  and greens

Preheat a fan oven to 160°C (320°F/gas 4).

Heat the oil over a medium heat in a large flameproof casserole dish (Dutch oven). Add the chicken and fry for 5–7 minutes on both sides until the skin is starting to crisp.

Add the onion and fry for a further 7 minutes until soft then add the apricot halves and fry for another 3 minutes until they start to soften too.

Stir in the miso paste and cook for 1 minute. Turn up the heat and pour in the cider. Bring to the boil for 1 minute, then take off the heat.

Transfer the casserole dish, uncovered, to the oven and cook for 20 minutes until the chicken is tender and cooked through.

While the chicken is in the oven, toast the pine nuts in a dry non-stick frying pan (skillet) for 5 minutes, stirring regularly, until lightly browned.

Remove the chicken from the oven, garnish with the chopped parsley and toasted pine nuts and serve with your favourite veg and greens.

Chicken with cider

Creamy chicken and cider with chunks of sweet caramelised apple is a cheering and comforting combination. I like chicken thighs best for this dish but other cuts will work, too. Served with either steamed vegetables or rice, this dish is simple, easy to prepare and will have your guests clamouring for more!

Serves 4
Prep 10 mins
Cook 50 mins

80 g (3 oz) butter
8 skin-on, bone-in
  chicken thighs
150 g (5 oz) shallots, chopped
2 garlic cloves, sliced
500 ml (17 fl oz/2 cups)
  dry cider
2 tablespoons
  wholegrain mustard
2 tablespoons chopped
  tarragon leaves
2 crisp, sweet eating (dessert)
  apples, such as Cox's
  or Chivers Delight, cored
  and cut into 8 wedges
salt and freshly ground
  black pepper
150 g (5 oz/⅔ cup)
  crème fraîche

To serve
your choice of vegetables

Line a plate with paper towels. Heat 30 g (1 oz) of the butter in a large frying pan (skillet) until hot. Add the chicken to the pan skin-side down, then cook over a medium-high heat for 5–8 minutes until brown all over and the skin is crisp. Turn and cook on the other side for a couple more minutes then, once cooked, set aside on the prepared plate.

Add a further 30 g (1 oz) of the butter to the pan along with the shallots and garlic and fry for 2–3 minutes until browned.

Increase the heat to high, pour in the cider and bring to the boil, then boil for 1 minute. Reduce the heat to low and stir in the wholegrain mustard and half the tarragon leaves. Return the chicken to the pan and simmer gently for 30 minutes.

Meanwhile, heat the remaining butter in a separate pan until quite hot. Add the apple pieces and fry for 2–4 minutes until the apple begin to soften and caramelise. Once cooked, take off the heat.

Season the chicken with salt and pepper and stir in the crème fraîche. Simmer for a further 5 minutes without letting the liquid boil.

Add the caramelised apple and garnish with the last of the tarragon leaves. Serve with your favourite vegetables.

Roast duck and cider brandy sauce

Roast duck is packed with flavour and gives as good as it gets when paired with Somerset cider brandy. If you aren't able to find cider brandy then regular brandy works here too. Cooking the duck in an intense heat, breast-side up, will help to give you lovely crispy skin as well as keeping the meat lovely and moist.

Serves 4

Prep 5 mins

Cook 1 hour 5 minutes

1 large duck

salt and freshly ground
  black pepper

1 cinnamon stick

1 teaspoon cloves

1 teaspoon peppercorns

3 crisp, sharp eating (dessert)
  apples, such as Granny
  Smith or Red Fastaff, cored
  and cut into wedges

2 tablespoons runny honey

100 ml (3½ fl oz/scant
  ½ cup) dry cider

juice of ½ lemon

150 ml (5 fl oz/scant
  ⅔ cup) Somerset cider
  brandy or brandy

Preheat a fan oven to 220°C (425°F/gas 9). Dry the duck skin well with a paper towel and season generously with salt and pepper.

Place the duck, breast-side down, in a roasting pan and roast in the oven for 25 minutes. Take the duck out of the oven and turn it over breast-side up. Baste the duck in the fat.

Reduce the oven temperature to 180°C (350°F/gas 6). Baste the duck once more and drain off any excess fat, leaving about 1 cm (½ in) in the base of the pan.

Add the cinnamon stick, cloves, peppercorns and apple wedges to the roasting pan. Smother the breast skin in the honey and pour the cider and lemon juice over the duck. Place back in the oven for a further 30 minutes, basting a couple times during cooking.

Remove the roasting pan from the oven and check the duck is cooked. The juices should run clear when you pierce the thickest part of the leg. Remove the duck and apples from the tray and place to one side to rest.

Heat the roasting pan on the hob and bring the fat and juices to a vigorous simmer. Add the brandy and allow the alcohol to burn off for 2–3 minutes, stirring. You may need to add more fat here too to make the sauce thick and glossy.

Slice the duck, arrange on a serving plate and garnish with the apple wedges. Pour a little sauce over the top, then serve the rest separately.

Spiced pumpkin, apple and cider stew

Deeply spiced and packed with winter root vegetables and nutritious kale, this vegetarian stew provides a warming and wholesome meal for the whole family. Served with rice, but equally delicious with crusty bread too.

Serves 4
Prep 15 mins
Cook 1 hour

2 tablespoons olive oil
1 medium onion, peeled
  and chopped
450 g (1 lb) pumpkin
  or squash, peeled and
  chopped into 2.5 cm
  (1 in) cubes
150 g (5 oz) new potatoes,
  chopped in half
150 g (5 oz) carrots, peeled
  and chopped into 2.5 cm
  (1 in) chunks
1 medium Bramley or Granny
  Smith apple
2 garlic cloves
1 cm (½ in) piece of ginger
½ teaspoon ground coriander
½ teaspoon ground cinnamon
½ teaspoon paprika
1 teaspoon chilli flakes
1 teaspoon cumin seeds
500 ml (17 fl oz/2 cups)
  dry cider
300 ml (10 fl oz/1¼ cups)
  vegetable stock
50 g (2 oz) raisins
100 g (3½ oz) kale
salt and freshly ground
  black pepper

To serve
rice or crusty bread
  and butter

Heat the oil on a medium heat in a large pan. Then, add the onion and fry for 2 minutes until it begins to soften. Add the pumpkin, new potatoes and carrots and cook for 5 minutes until the vegetables begin to softening at the edges.

Add the apple, garlic and ginger and fry for a further 2 minutes. Stir in the coriander, cinnamon, paprika, chilli flakes and cumin seeds, ensuring that the vegetables are well coated, and fry for 3–5 minutes.

Increase the heat and pour in the cider. Bring to the boil before adding the vegetable stock and raisins. Cover and reduce the heat to a light simmer then cook on a low heat for 45 minutes or until the vegetables are cooked through.

Once the vegetables are cooked, stir in the kale and cook for a further 3 minutes so that the kale is cooked through, but still a little crunchy in the stem. Season to taste with salt and pepper, then serve with some rice or thick crusty bread and butter.

Chicken, cider and Cheddar crumble

The three Cs crumble! This makes for a warming, wholesome supper and can be made ahead of time and chilled until needed. Just leave the final baking until about half an hour before you want to serve.

Serves 6
Prep 20 mins
Cook 40 mins

2 tablespoons olive oil
1 large onion, chopped
2 celery stalks, chopped
2 carrots, chopped
2 garlic cloves, crushed
100 g (3½ oz) mushrooms,
   sliced
350 g (12 oz) skinless
   boneless chicken thighs,
   cut into chunks
1 teaspoon dried oregano
1 cooking apple, such as a
   Bramley, peeled and cored
1 tablespoon wholegrain
   mustard
200 ml (7 fl oz/scant 1 cup)
   dry cider
100 g (3½ oz/scant ½ cup)
   crème fraîche
salt and freshly ground
   black pepper

For the crumble
250 g (9 oz/2 cups) plain
   (all-purpose) flour
1 teaspoon mustard powder
salt and freshly ground
   black pepper
150 g (5 oz) butter, at room
   temperature, diced
150 g (5 oz) mature Cheddar,
   grated (shredded)
30 g (1 oz/¼ cup)
   hazelnuts, chopped

To serve
your choice of vegetables

Preheat a fan oven to 180°C (350°F/gas 6).

Heat the oil in a large frying pan (skillet) over a medium heat and fry the onion, celery and carrots for 5 minutes until they begin to soften. Add the garlic and mushrooms and fry for a further 3 minutes.

Add the chicken and oregano to the pan and continue frying for another 10 minutes until the chicken has cooked through and is beginning to brown. Cut the apple into 8 wedges, add to the pan and fry for a further 2 minutes.

Next, add the mustard and stir in well. Then pour in the cider and increase the heat. Cook on a high heat for 3–5 minutes until the alcohol has burnt off and liquid has reduced by about a quarter. Turn off the heat, stir in the crème fraîche and season to taste with salt and pepper. Then transfer to a large baking dish.

To make the crumble topping, put the flour, mustard powder and some salt and pepper in a bowl and mix together. Add the butter, then rub between your fingers and thumbs until you have a breadcrumb-like mixture. Stir in the cheese and hazelnuts and mix well.

Top the apple, chicken and cider with the crumble and bake in the oven for 25 minutes until the crumble is golden brown and crunchy. Serve with your favourite vegetables.

Turkey and apple burgers

Turkey recipes are for all year round – not just for Christmas – and this delicate meat goes so well with sweet apple. You can also use minced (ground) pork here, or even lamb or beef. Serve with the Ultimate apple sauce (page 128) or Apple and chilli jelly (page 120).

Serves 4
Prep 10 mins + chilling
Cook 15–20 mins

350 g (12 oz) minced (ground) turkey
small bunch of thyme, leaves removed and finely chopped
2 sweet, juicy eating (dessert) apples, such as Cox's, peeled, cored and finely chopped
½ teaspoon chilli (hot pepper) flakes
salt and freshly ground black pepper
1 egg, beaten
a little plain (all-purpose) flour, for dusting
1 tablespoon vegetable oil
1 onion, sliced

To serve
butter, for spreading
4 brioche or burger buns, halved
1 little gem (bibb) lettuce
2 ripe vine tomatoes, sliced
burger sauces or chutneys or Ultimate apple sauce (page 128) or Apple and chilli jelly (page 120)

Mix the turkey, thyme and apple in a bowl, stir in the chilli flakes and season with salt and pepper. Add the egg and mix everything well to combine.

Wet your hands a little to stop the turkey and apple mixture from sticking to them, then take a quarter of the mixture and mould it into a patty in your hands. Repeat to make 4 burgers in total. Dust a little flour on each side of the burgers, then pop them in the refrigerator to chill and firm up for 30 minutes before cooking.

Heat the oil over a medium heat in a large frying pan (skillet). Fry the burgers for 3–5 minutes on each side until cooked through and golden and crispy on the outside. Remove from the pan and leave to rest on a plate lined with paper towels.

While the burgers are resting, fry the onion over a medium heat in the frying pan (skillet) until caramelised and cooked through. You might need a touch more oil.

Finally, assemble your burgers by buttering your brioche buns, adding the burgers, lettuce leaves, tomato slices, onion and your favourite burger sauces, chutneys or a hearty dollop of the ultimate apple sauce or apple and chilli jelly.

Rabbit and cider stew

Rabbit stew is a delicious way to celebrate the autumn. The rich gamey flavours of rabbit and the fruity cider flavour work really well in this dish – warming for the heart and soul as the colder, darker nights draw in. Preferably, use wild rabbit here, if you can get it and it is in season.

Serves 4
Prep 15 mins
Cook 2 hours 10 mins

2 tablespoons olive oil
6 slices of smoked bacon,
  cut into 1 cm (½ in) strips
1 large rabbit, jointed
20 g (¾ oz) butter
150 g (5 oz) shallots, sliced
2 garlic cloves, sliced
12 baby carrots
175 g (6 oz) wild
  mushrooms, chopped
1 teaspoon juniper berries
½ teaspoon black peppercorns
2 tablespoons runny honey
1 sprig of thyme
2 bay leaves
500 ml (17 fl oz/2 cups)
  dry cider
150 g (5 oz) frozen peas
2 tablespoons crème fraîche
  (optional)

Preheat a fan oven to 140°C (280°F/gas 3).

Heat the oil in a flameproof casserole dish (Dutch over) over a medium heat. Add the bacon and fry for about 3 minutes until it begins to go brown. Fry the rabbit pieces in batches, sealing each side for 1–2 minutes to brown. Remove with a slotted spoon to a side plate to rest.

Melt the butter in the same dish and add the shallots. Cook for 2–3 minutes until they begin to sweat. Add the garlic and carrots and cook for a further 5 minutes, ensuring nothing burns.

Then, add the mushrooms, juniper berries, peppercorns and mix well. Cook for 3 minutes to allow the flavours to start to come together. Stir in the honey and return the rabbit pieces to the pan.

Add the thyme and bay leaves and pour the cider over the top. Bring to boiling point, then reduce to a simmer.

Cover the dish and cook in the oven for 1 hour 45 minutes.

Take the dish out of the oven and return to the hob over a low heat. Stir in the peas, then cover and cook for 5 minutes. Finally, stir through the crème fraîche, if using, and serve.

Braised pork knuckles in cider

You could say that pork and apple have had an eternal love affair. They just work so well together. The meaty pork flavour and the sweet, yet sharp tang of apples is a dream combination, which is even better when you get the crackling just right! Pork knuckles are a more unusual cut of meat. On the bone, you will most likely need to ask your butcher for it as supermarkets have yet to catch on to this utterly tantalising and very cheap cut.

The most important thing with knuckle is time: make sure you have plenty of it to slow cook the joint to allow for the meat to absorb and infuse with that delicious cider.

Serves 4
Prep 15 mins + resting
Cook 3 hours 10 mins

1 tablespoon salt flakes
1 teaspoon caraway seeds
3 garlic cloves, crushed
1 sprig of rosemary
2 pork knuckles (ask your
   butcher to score the rind)
2 onions, sliced
2 sweet eating (dessert) apples,
   such as Braeburn or Cox's,
   peeled, cored and sliced
500 ml (17 fl oz/2 cups) dry
   scrumpy or cider
250 ml (8½ fl oz/1 cup)
   boiling water

To serve
roast potatoes
spring greens

Preheat a fan oven to 220°C (425°F/gas 9).

Make a rub by combining the salt, caraway seeds, garlic and rosemary in a pestle and mortar, crushing to release and combine all those delicious flavours from the caraway and rosemary. Rub the mix into the pork knuckles, ensuring you get fully into the scored rind.

Arrange the onions and apples in layers in a large roasting pan. Pop the knuckles on top and cook in the oven for 40 minutes.

Take the pan out of the oven, pour half the cider over the knuckles and add the boiling water to the pan. Reduce the oven temperature to 170°C (340°F/gas 5) and cook in the oven for a further 2 hours until the knuckles are really tender.

Remove from the oven and pour the remaining cider over the knuckles. Return the oven temperature to 220°C (425°F/gas 9) and roast the pork for a further 30 minutes until the skin is nicely crackled.

Take the knuckles out of the oven and remove from the pan, cover lightly in foil and leave to rest for at least 15 minutes.

While the knuckles are resting, heat the pan, with all the juices, on the hob until they begin to bubble. Mash the onions and apples together and boil to reduce slightly until you have a thick gravy. Pour or strain into a gravy jug.

Serve the pork knuckles and gravy alongside some roast potatoes and spring greens.

Spicy pork chops with cider vinegar sauce

I love pork chops. When I hear people complain about them being dry and tasteless, I'm sure of one thing: they just ain't cookin' 'em right! This recipe has everything to make pork chops succulent and delicious: sour from the barberries or juniper berries and sweetness from the apples, with the cider and chilli complementing the flavours beautifully. Once you cook this, you'll never have a 'dry, tasteless' pork chop again – and that's a promise.

Serves 4
Prep 10 mins
Cook 50–55 mins

4 thick pork chops, with
   the bone and plenty of fat,
   if possible
salt and freshly ground
   black pepper
1 tablespoon olive oil
10 g (¼ oz) butter
1 large onion, sliced
3 large, crisp eating (dessert)
   apples, such as Russet or
   Granny Smith, cored and
   cut into wedges
2 tablespoons shop-bought
   or homemade Apple cider
   vinegar (page 133)
1 teaspoon fresh thyme leaves
2 dried red chillies, halved
1 teaspoon barberries,
   dried barberries or dried
   juniper berries
200 ml (7 fl oz/scant 1 cup)
   dry cider

To serve
Apple and red cabbage slaw
   (page 105) or roast potatoes
   and stir-fried tenderstem
   broccoli

Preheat a fan oven to 200°C (400°F/gas 8).

Season the chops with salt and pepper. Heat the oil in a large, flameproof casserole dish (Dutch oven) until hot and fry the chops, starting with the fatty rind to begin to get it nice and crispy. Hold each chop rind-side down for about a minute each before sealing the other sides briefly in the oil. Remove from the dish and set aside.

Melt the butter in the dish and add the onion. Fry for 3–5 minutes until the onion begins to go translucent. Then, add the apple wedges and fry for a further 2–3 minutes until the apple begins to caramelise.

Add the cider vinegar and heat in the dish for 1 minute, scraping any sticky goodness from the bottom with a wooden spoon. Toss in the thyme, chillies and barberries.

Finally, return the chops to the dish and pour the cider over the top. Bring to the boil, then transfer to the hot oven. Cook in the oven for 35 minutes until the meat is tender and succulent and the sauce is thick. Serve with apple slaw or roast potatoes and stir-fried tenderstem broccoli.

Slow-cooked pork and cider

Pork cooked very slowly in a cider alongside a selection of vegetables and herbs makes a delicious, and actually very easy to prepare, meal. Plus, pork and cider only get better when you cook the dish a day ahead, and it freezes beautifully – just omit the crème fraîche until you're ready to reheat and serve.

Serves 4
Prep 10 mins
Cook 2 hours 30 mins

50 g (2 oz) butter
150 g (5 oz) smoked
  bacon lardons
1 kg (2 lb 4 oz) pork
  shoulder, excess fat
  removed and chopped
  into 2.5 cm (1 in) chunks
salt and freshly ground
  black pepper
1 large onion, sliced
2 celery stalks, cut into
  2 cm (¾ in) chunks
2 carrots, peeled and chopped
  into 2 cm (¾ in) chunks
small handful of fresh
  sage leaves
1 teaspoon juniper berries
2 crisp, sweet eating (dessert)
  apples, such as Cox's
  or Chivers Delight, cored
  and cut into wedges
500 ml (17 fl oz/2 cups)
  dry cider, ideally
  traditional scrumpy
300 ml (10 fl oz/1¼ cups)
  chicken stock
2 tablespoons wholegrain
  mustard
4 tablespoons crème fraîche

To serve
steamed new potatoes
greens

Preheat a fan oven to 140°C (280°F/gas 3).

Put half the butter in a large, flameproof casserole dish (Dutch oven) over a medium heat. Add the lardons and fry for a couple minutes until they brown and start to crisp up. Remove with a slotted spoon and set aside.

Add the pork to the casserole dish, in batches, and season generously with salt and pepper. Fry until the pork is brown all over and also beginning to crisp on the edges. Set aside with the lardons.

Add the rest of the butter to the dish and melt with the fat from the meat, turning down the heat to medium-low. Add the onion and fry for 1–2 minutes until beginning to soften and brown before throwing in the celery and carrots. Stir thoroughly and allow to fry together in the fat for a good 5 minutes until softened and just beginning to brown. Add the sage, juniper berries and apple wedges and stir for another minute.

Increase the heat slightly and return the pork and lardons back to the dish. Stir everything together.

Pour in the cider and bring to the boil for 2 minutes, then add the stock and reduce to a simmer, ensuring everything is mixed in well. Put the lid on the casserole dish and pop in the oven for 2 hours.

Return the casserole dish to the hob, remove the lid and give everything a good stir. The vegetables and meat should be tender and succulent. Next, heat to a simmer and let it bubble gently for 5–10 minutes until the liquid has reduced to two-thirds its original volume.

Stir in the mustard. (At this point you can leave the casserole dish to cool and freeze or keep in the refrigerator for a couple days before reheating to serve.)

Finally, stir in the crème fraîche and serve with steamed new potatoes and greens.

Slow-roasted pork belly and pickled apple

This slow-roasted pork belly is mouth-wateringly juicy, with perfect crackling, and makes a scrumptious supper, served with potatoes and a coleslaw or salad, but equally good carved into slices to enjoy the next day in a sandwich made with crusty bread and a spoonful of my Ultimate apple sauce (page 128). Pork-fection!

Serves 6

Prep 20 mins

Cook 3 hours 15 mins –
   3 hours 25 mins

1 kg (2 lb 4 oz) piece of pork
   belly (get your butcher
   to score the skin)
a couple pinches
   of sea salt flakes
150 ml (5 fl oz/scant
   ⅔ cup) dark soy sauce
200 ml (7 fl oz/scant 1 cup)
   dry cider
250 ml (8½ fl oz/1 cup) water
2 star anise
½ teaspoon Chinese
   five-spice powder

For the cider pickle

150 ml (5 fl oz/scant
   ⅔ cup) shop-bought
   or homemade Apple cider
   vinegar (page 133)
100 g (3½ oz/scant ½ cup)
   caster (superfine) sugar
4 cloves
1 tablespoon salt
2 sweet eating (dessert)
   apples, such as Braeburn

To serve

salad or your choice
   of vegetables

Preheat a fan oven to 160°C (320°F/gas 4).

Put the pork belly in a roasting pan and dry with a paper towel. Then, rub with a pinch of sea salt flakes and leave to stand.

In a bowl, combine the soy sauce, cider, water, star anise and Chinese five-spice. Pour over the pork and make sure the meat, but not the skin, is mostly covered. Cover with foil and cook in the oven for 2 hours 45 minutes, basting the skin halfway through. The pork should be beautifully tender.

Remove the foil, baste the skin in the fragrant liquid once again and sprinkle over a pinch of sea salt flakes. Pour the excess liquid into a separate bowl and discard. Increase the oven temperature to 200°C (400°F/gas 8) and roast the pork belly for 30–40 minutes to help the skin crackle up. Keep an eye on the meat and don't let it burn. Remove from the oven and let it stand for 30 minutes.

While the pork is cooking, make the pickle. Heat the cider vinegar, sugar and cloves in a saucepan with the salt to make a brine. Simmer until the sugar has completely dissolved. Remove from the heat and leave to cool completely.

Once the brine has cooled, core and slice the apple, leaving the skin on. Pour the brine over the apple until it is completely covered and let it pickle stand for 15 minutes.

Carve the pork belly finely and serve alongside the pickled apple and a salad or some of your favourite veg.

Pork loin with mustard and apples

Pork loin and apples with a generous spread of mustard is a simple meal – all it takes is a little time, but it is very much worth the wait to enjoy those caramelised almost chutney-like apples slathered in mustard sauce and pork juices.

Serves 4
Prep 10 mins
Cook 1 hour

1 tablespoon olive oil
600 g (1 lb 5 oz) pork loin
1 onion, sliced
2 teaspoons dried thyme
2 garlic cloves, thinly sliced
4 sweet eating (dessert)
    apples, such as Fiesta or
    Cox's, cored and quartered
2 tablespoons Somerset
    cider brandy
3 tablespoons wholegrain
    mustard
150 ml (5 fl oz/scant
    ⅔ cup) chicken stock

To serve
steamed kale
new potatoes

Preheat a fan oven to 180°C (350°F/gas 6).

Heat the olive oil in a flameproof casserole dish (Dutch oven). When the oil is hot, fry the pork loin for 2 minutes on each side to seal. The loin will be nicely golden in colour. Remove the loin and pop it on a plate to rest.

Add the onion to the dish and fry for 3 minutes until soft. Add the thyme, garlic and apple quarters and fry for a further 5 minutes until the apples are starting to soften.

Increase the heat, add the cider brandy and simmer for a few minutes until the alcohol is cooked off. Add the mustard and chicken stock, stirring well, and reduce to a simmer. Return the pork loin to the dish and simmer for 2–3 minutes before placing the dish in the oven. Cook for 40 minutes until the pork is tender. Check the pork is cooked properly by cutting into the thickest part of the meat – it should be pale in colour (not pink) and the juices should run clear. If it is not cooked through, return it to the oven for a further 10 minutes, or until it is ready.

Place the cooked pork on a chopping board to rest and cover with foil to keep warm.

Put the dish back on the hob over a medium heat, bring back to the boil, then simmer until the liquid is reduced to a gravy-like consistency. Carve the pork loin and serve with the mustard glaze alongside some steamed kale and new potatoes.

Sweet and sticky ribs with apple wedges

Who doesn't love sweet, sticky ribs? And the sugars in the apple juice make these even more sticky and even more moreish. Yes, ribs are a messy affair, but you'll be hearing no complaints from your fellow diners. In fact, you'll probably not be hearing much from them at all! Cooking the ribs in a saucepan with all the liquid ingredients before putting them in the oven helps keep them perfectly moist as well as cutting down the cooking time for what is usually a slow-cook dish.

Serves 6
Prep 15 mins
Cook 1 hour 10 mins

1 litre (34 fl oz/4 cups) cloudy
  apple juice
150 ml (5 fl oz/scant
  ⅔ cup) shop-bought
  or homemade Apple cider
  vinegar (page 133)
350 ml (12¼ fl oz/1½ cups)
  water
2 bay leaves
2 tablespoons salt
1 cinnamon stick
2 star anise
2 teaspoon black peppercorns
2 kg (4 lb 8 oz) pork ribs
2 sharp, green eating
  (dessert) apples, such
  as Granny Smith, cored
  and cut into wedges

For the sticky sauce
100 ml (3½ fl oz/scant
  ½ cup) Apple syrup
  (page 116) or runny honey
2 tablespoons
  Worcestershire sauce
2 garlic cloves,
  grated (shredded)
1 onion, chopped

To serve
Apple and red cabbage slaw
  (page 105) or green salad

Put the apple juice, cider vinegar, water, bay leaves, salt, cinnamon stick, star anise and black peppercorns into a large saucepan and bring to the boil. Once boiling, add the ribs and reduce the heat to a simmer for 30 minutes.

Preheat a fan oven to 200°C (400°F/gas 8).

Take the ribs out of the liquid and place in a large roasting pan. Pour enough of the liquid from the saucepan into the roasting pan to almost cover the ribs to keep them moist.

Next, make the sticky sauce by adding the apple syrup or honey, Worcestershire sauce, garlic, onion and 500 ml (17 fl oz/2 cups) of the apple juice liquid into a saucepan. Bring to the boil, then simmer until the liquid has reduced by about one-third and is thick and very sticky.

Next, lift the ribs out of their cooking liquid and reserve the liquid (you might need it later). Pour the sticky sauce over the ribs and turn so that are coated in the sauce. Add the apple wedges to the pan and roast with the ribs for 30-40 minutes, turning midway through, until the ribs are dark and almost blackened. Check regularly to make sure they do not burn – add a little of the reserved liquid to the pan if necessary.

When the ribs are ready, serve with some Apple and red cabbage slaw or a green salad.

Cider-glazed ham

A glazed ham is a must at Christmas time – something that can be made ahead of time and brought out to an appreciative audience. Cooking the meat in cider and then roasting with honey gives it a lovely sweet and fragrant flavour. I prefer cooking ham on the bone – it's more impressive on the table, in my opinion – however you can easily make this with boneless gammon too. You can also use unsmoked gammon, if you prefer.

Serves 10
Prep 20 mins + standing
Cook 2 hours 10 mins

2.5 kg (5 lb 10 oz) smoked
 gammon, on the bone
1 onion, quartered
1 carrot, chopped into
 large chunks
2 bay leaves
1 sprig of rosemary
1 teaspoon black peppercorns
1 teaspoon juniper berries
750 ml (25 fl oz/3 cups)
 dry cider
4 tablespoons runny honey
2 tablespoons
 wholegrain mustard
2 tablespoons cloves
1 tablespoon soft light
 brown sugar
1 orange, sliced

Put the gammon joint, onion, carrot, bay leaves, rosemary, black peppercorns and juniper berries into a large ovenproof saucepan. Pour over 500 ml (17 fl oz/2 cups) of the cider, then fill the pan with water to just cover the ham. Cover with the lid and heat on the hob until boiling, then reduce to a simmer for 1 hour 30 minutes. Skim off any scum as it cooks.

Preheat a fan oven to 180°C (350°F/gas 6). While the ham is cooking, mix the honey with the mustard.

When the ham is cooked, transfer it to a roasting pan and leave to cool for 10 minutes. When the ham is cool enough to handle, remove the rind carefully, ensuring you keep as much of the soft fat underneath with the ham. Score the soft fat in a criss-cross pattern.

Stud the ham with the whole cloves and pour over the rest of the cider. Then, using a basting brush, brush the honey and mustard all over the ham, making sure you cover the entire joint. Sprinkle with the brown sugar. Finally, arrange the orange slices over the top.

Roast in the oven for 30–40 minutes, basting a couple times to keep it moist. You want the ham to be nicely browned and almost starting to blacken. Remove from the oven and let it stand for at least 20 minutes before carving.

Sides and Sauces

From sweet jam and jelly to spicy chutney, in salads or slaws or just simply pickled and served raw, apples make wonderful and varied sidekicks to many dishes. Savoury to sweet, their sharp and sometimes tangy flavours can help elevate other dishes and transform flavour combinations.

Apple and red cabbage slaw

A vibrant and crisp salad that makes an excellent addition to some leftover roast chicken or to serve with the Sweet and sticky ribs on page 96.

Serves 2

Prep 10 mins

2 tablespoons shop-bought or homemade Apple cider vinegar (page 133)

1 tablespoon runny honey

2 teaspoons wholegrain mustard

2 teaspoons extra virgin olive oil

salt and freshly ground black pepper

1 crisp green eating (dessert) apple, such as Granny Smith, cored and sliced into matchsticks

200 g (7 oz) red cabbage, centre removed and leaves thinly sliced or grated

1 large orange or red (bell) pepper, deseeded and thinly sliced into matchsticks

1 carrot, cut into matchsticks

2 spring onions (scallions), cut into matchsticks

25 g (1 oz) coriander (cilantro), stalks removed and leaves chopped

Whisk together the cider vinegar, honey, mustard and oil in a small bowl. Season with some salt and pepper and put to one side.

Put the apple, red cabbage, pepper, carrot, spring onions and coriander in a large salad bowl and mix together.

When you're ready to serve, drizzle over the dressing and toss the veggies and apple through to coat evenly.

Apple bread

Delicately spiced with cinnamon and nutmeg, this apple bread makes delicious toast for breakfast, but also goes surprisingly well with cheese and Apple membrillo (page 124).

Makes 1
Prep 20 mins
Bake 1 hour

175 g (6 oz/scant 1½ cups)
  strong white bread flour
¾ teaspoon baking powder
150 g (5 oz/⅔ cup) caster
  (superfine) sugar
½ teaspoon salt
½ teaspoon ground cinnamon
¼ teaspoon freshly
  grated nutmeg
120 ml (4 fl oz/½ cup)
  vegetable oil
2 eggs, beaten
¼ teaspoon vanilla extract
2 large crisp eating (dessert)
  apples, such as Cox's or
  Granny Smith, peeled,
  cored and cut into 1 cm
  (¾ in) cubes

Preheat a fan oven to 160°C (320°F/gas 4) and grease a 450 g (1 lb) loaf pan with butter and line with baking parchment.

Into an electric mixer, sift together the flour and baking powder. Add the sugar, salt, cinnamon and nutmeg and mix on a medium speed until combined.

Slowly add the vegetable oil, a little at a time, mixing well between each addition. Then mix in the eggs and vanilla extract.

When everything is combined, gently fold in the apple chunks. Transfer the apple dough to the loaf pan and bake in the oven for 1 hour or until a knife inserted in the middle comes out clean.

Remove from the oven and leave to cool slightly in the pan before turning out onto a wire rack. Serve toasted with some butter and a nice cup of tea.

Apple, thyme and Cheddar scones

The flavours of the sweet apple and savoury, herby thyme blend nicely together in these aromatic scones, while the saltiness of extra mature Cheddar cuts through to provide a tasty bite. These scones are best served fresh and warm out of the oven.

Makes 8–10
Prep 20 mins
Cook 15–20 mins

200 g (7 oz/scant 1⅔ cups)
   self-raising flour, plus extra
   for dusting
2 teaspoons mustard powder
2 teaspoons baking powder
1 teaspoon dried thyme
½ teaspoon salt
100 g (3½ oz) cold butter,
   grated (shredded)
150 g (5 oz) Cheddar, finely
   grated (shredded)
2 sharp eating (dessert)
   apples, such as Cox's, cored
   and grated (shredded)
2 eggs, beaten
3 tablespoons whole milk,
   plus extra for brushing

Preheat a fan oven to 190°C (375°F/gas 7) and line a large baking sheet with baking parchment.

Mix together the flour, mustard powder, baking powder, thyme and salt until well combined. Add the butter and rub the mixture together with your fingertips until evenly combined.

Stir the cheese and apples into the mixture.

Mix the beaten eggs and milk together and gradually work into the flour mixture until you have a firm but moist dough. Roll out the dough on a lightly floured work surface until it is about 2.5 cm (1 in) thick all over. Cut out the dough using a 80 mm (3 in) cutter – you should get at least 8 scones and maybe a couple more and brush with milk.

Put on the prepared baking sheet and bake in the oven for 15–20 minutes, watching closely so that they don't overbake. Serve immediately.

Apple bread (106)

Apple, thyme and
Cheddar scones (107)

Apple crisps

A slightly different take on the traditional crispy-chips snack but equally moreish. Perfect for adding to granola (page 38) or as a substitute to crisps (chips).

Serves 2
Prep 5 mins
Cook 40 mins

2 sharp eating (dessert) apples, such as Cox's
pinch of sea salt flakes

Preheat a fan oven to 140°C (280°F/gas 3) and line a baking sheet with baking parchment.

Slice the apples very finely, ideally using a mandolin to get evenly sliced apple.

Place them in a single layer on the lined baking sheet and bake in the oven for 40 minutes until slightly golden.

Remove from the oven and leave to cool until crisp.

Finally, sprinkle with sea salt flakes and serve. Store in an airtight container for up to 3 days.

Apple and tomato relish

Apples and tomatoes are packed with lively, bold flavours and, when paired together in chutney or relishes, create something really quite special – the ideal accompaniment for some strong cheese, a pork pie or spread generously inside a hearty ham sandwich. I prefer to leave the skins on the apples when I make this, but you can peel them if you prefer.

Makes about 1.5 kg
  (3 lb 5 oz)
Prep 15 mins
Cook 1 hour 30 mins

1 kg (2 lb 4 oz) very ripe
  beef tomatoes, skinned
  and chopped
600 g (1 lb 5 oz) cooking
  apples, such as Bramleys,
  cored and chopped
300 g (10½ oz) shallots,
  chopped
2 celery stalks, chopped
3 bird's eye chillies, deseeded
  and finely chopped
1 tablespoon fennel seeds
1 tablespoon smoked paprika
250 ml (8½ fl oz/1 cup) water
1 litre (34 fl oz/4 cups) Apple
  cider vinegar
200 g (7 oz/scant 1¼ cups)
  light soft brown sugar
1 tablespoon salt

Prepare and sterilise 12 jars (page 27).

Put the tomatoes, apples, shallots, celery, chillies, fennel seeds, paprika and water in a large saucepan over a medium heat and bring to the boil. Reduce the heat, cover with a lid and simmer for 30 minutes until the vegetables are soft.

Add the vinegar, sugar and salt and simmer very gently for a further 1 hour, uncovered, stirring regularly. Most of the liquid needs to evaporate so you may need more time depending on how juicy the tomatoes were. Keep a close eye on it, though, as you don't want it to stick.

Once you have a thick consistency, remove the pan from the heat. While the chutney is still hot, transfer it to the prepared jars, then seal and label them with the name and the date. The relish will last at least 6 months unopened or 1 month in the refrigerator once opened.

Somerset apple chutney

This chutney is an old recipe that is based on my favourite traditional version, but with the addition of ginger, cayenne and turmeric. It is a dark, tasty chutney that goes particularly well with strong Cheddar.

Makes about 2 kg (4 lb 8 oz)
Prep 20 mins
Cook 1 hour 10 mins

1 kg (2 lb 4 oz) cooking
  apples, such as Bramleys,
  peeled, cored and chopped
600 g (1 lb 5 oz) onions,
  finely chopped
2 preserved lemons, thinly
  sliced and pips removed
200 g (7 oz/scant
  1⅔ cups) raisins
3 garlic cloves, chopped
500 ml (17 fl oz/
  2 cups) shop-bought
  or homemade Apple cider
  vinegar (page 133)
400 g (14 oz) black treacle
  (dark molasses)
1 tablespoon salt
½ teaspoon cayenne pepper
1 teaspoon ground turmeric

To serve
slice of Cheddar
crusty bread
your choice of fruit
  and nuts

Prepare and sterilise 12 jars (page 27).

Put the apples, onions, preserved lemons, raisins, garlic and vinegar in a large, heavy-based saucepan and bring to the boil. Reduce the heat and simmer for 20 minutes until the apples are soft but not broken up.

Stir in the treacle and simmer for 45 minutes until the liquid has reduced and you have a chutney-like consistency.

Stir in the salt and spices and continue heating for another 2 minutes until everything is mixed in well. Take off the heat and decant into the prepared jars. Serve with a hefty slice of Cheddar, some crusty bread and some fruit and nuts. Store in a cool, dry place until opened, then keep in the refrigerator. It will keep for up to 3 months.

Apple syrup

Apple syrup – or *appelstroop* – is hugely popular in the Netherlands and other parts of northern Europe, but barely known in other countries (especially the UK, which is odd given we're only across the Channel!). It's made by reducing good-quality apple juice with lemon juice and spices until you get a thick, dark syrup that can be used for everything from savoury dishes and salad dressings to pastries and even as an alternative to jam (jelly) or served with some yoghurt and fruit for breakfast as photographed. It's really quite adaptable and has an utterly delicious tart and fruity flavour. Personally, I think appelstroop comes into its own when used in savoury dishes: hot pots, stews and soups. It elevates other ingredients and deepens the flavour of the dish. I would seriously encourage you to give it a try – you can make it in batches and store it for a good few weeks in the refrigerator.

Makes about 250 ml
  (8½ fl oz/1 cup)
Prep 5 mins
Cook about 1 hour 30 mins

700 ml (24 fl oz/scant
  3 cups) good-quality, clear
  apple juice
2 teaspoons lemon juice
1 star anise
¼ teaspoon ground cinnamon
50 g (2 oz/scant ¼ cup) golden
  caster (superfine) sugar

Prepare and sterilise 1 or 2 jars (page 27).

Put the apple juice, lemon juice, star anise and ground cinnamon in a heavy-based saucepan and heat to simmer. Continue to boil until the liquid has reduced to about a quarter of its original quantity. This will take about an hour or perhaps more, so check on it regularly to make sure it doesn't burn on the bottom.

Once the syrup has reduced, take out the star anise and add the sugar, continuing to boil until the sugar has dissolved completely. The syrup will be ready when it has the consistency of honey.

Once ready, pour into the prepared jam jars, seal, label and leave to cool. The apple syrup may harden when it's completely cool, especially if refrigerated. If it does, then just heat up briefly in the microwave or pop the jar in a pot of warm water to soften before use.

Apple, rhubarb and ginger jam

Apple, rhubarb and ginger are great bedfellows – and are delicious in a crumble – but also in this light yet flavourful jam (jelly). It's something a little different to the usual jams and marmalades, but is just as tasty on toast.

Makes about 1.4 kg (3 lb)
Prep 20 mins
Cook 15 mins

400 g (14 oz) cooking apples, such as Bramleys, cored, peeled and chopped
350 g (12 oz) rhubarb, chopped into 1 cm (½ in) pieces
3 tablespoons water
1 cm (½ in) piece of ginger root, peeled and grated (shredded)
juice of 2 lemons
700 g (1 lb 9 oz/3 cups) caster (superfine) sugar

Prepare and sterilise 4 jars (page 27).

Put the apple, rhubarb and water in a large, heavy-based saucepan over a low heat for a couple minutes until the fruit starts to cook.

Add the ginger and lemon juice and then the sugar and turn up the heat until the sugar has dissolved.

Increase the temperature again and boil vigorously until the jam reaches 105°C (220°F) on a sugar thermometer or take a small spoonful of the jam and pour it onto a cold plate. Leave for a minute to cool and if the jam starts to set and crinkles if you gently push it, then it is ready.

Decant into the prepared jars, seal and label. Store in a cool, dry place until opened, then keep in the refrigerator. It will keep for up to 3 months.

Crab apple and blackberry jam

Apple and blackberry jam (jelly) is a winter favourite – making up and storing the best of the autumn flavours to savour throughout the shorter, colder months. This recipe uses crab apples, which have a slightly sweeter flavour than Bramley apples, but are actually brilliant for jam-making thanks to their high pectin level. If you can't find crab apples, however, then it is absolutely fine to use the equivalent weight of Bramley apples.

Makes about 1.5–2 kg
 (3 lb 5 oz–4 lb 8 oz)
Prep 15 mins
Cook 40 mins

650 g (1 lb 7 oz) crab apples,
 stalks removed
350 ml (12¼ fl oz/
 1½ cups) water
1 kg (2 lb 4 oz) blackberries
juice of 1 lemon
caster (superfine) sugar,
 equal to the weight of apple
 and blackberry once cooked

Prepare and sterilise 6 jars (page 27).

Put the apples and water in a large, heavy-based saucepan over a medium heat and bring to the boil, then reduce the heat and simmer for 5 minutes until the apple begins to soften.

Add the blackberries and lemon juice and cover, simmering for a further 15 minutes until everything is soft and mushy.

Carefully, weigh the warm apple and blackberry mixture, and return to the pan along with an equal weight of sugar. Bring to the boil and heat for 15 minutes, stirring continuously to allow the sugar to dissolve. Continue heating until a sugar thermometer reaches 105°C (220°F) or until a dollop of jam on a cold plate crinkles after a couple minutes of cooling.

Remove from the heat. Skim the top of the jam with a slotted spoon to remove any unwanted scum – there's nothing wrong with this but some people don't like it.

Decant into the prepared jars, seal and label. Once cool, the jam will keep for about 2 years.

Apple and mint jelly

Mint jelly is traditionally served with lamb, however this slightly sweeter version cooked with apple is delicious served with other meats, including pork, as well as melted in sauces and gravies. When preparing the apples, chop them up but leave the core in and peel on. This is where the most pectin is and will help give you a nicely set jelly.

Makes about 2–2.5 kg
  (4 lb 8 oz–5 lb oz)
Prep 10 mins + overnight
  straining
Cook 30 mins

2 kg (4 lb 8 oz) cooking apples,
  such as Bramleys, chopped
75 g (2½ oz) mint leaves
100 ml (3½ fl oz/scant
  ½ cup) shop-bought or
  homemade Apple cider
  vinegar (page 133)
caster (superfine) sugar,
  equal to half the weight
  of the juice

Prepare and sterilise 10 jars (page 271).

Put the apples and mint into a large, heavy-based saucepan and add just enough water to cover the apples. Bring to the boil over a medium heat, then reduce the heat and simmer for about 10 minutes until the apples break down.

Add the cider vinegar and bring back to the boil for 2 minutes. Remove from the heat.

Put the apple in a sieve (strainer) lined with muslin (cheesecloth) and let the juice drip into a bowl. This might take a while but don't be tempted to push it through to speed up the process. Let it take its time as this is how you get lovely clear jelly. Ideally, leave the apple dripping overnight.

When all the juice has dripped out, measure the amount of juice you have, and then measure out half as much sugar. Then, return the juice to the clean saucepan and add the sugar. Bring to the boil until the sugar has dissolved. Then continue to boil for about 15 minutes until the jelly reaches 105°C (220°F) on a sugar thermometer or when a few drops on a cold plate will wrinkle when pressed.

Once it reaches the desired heat, remove from the heat and decant into the prepared jars, seal and label. The jelly will keep for 1 year unopened.

Somerset cider marmalade

Apple and orange are bold and lively flavours and can work well together when managed carefully. The cider here gives the marmalade an aromatic, sweet tang that makes a tasty alternative to traditional marmalade and is delicious on toast or used as a glaze over ham.

Makes about 2 kg (4 lb 8 oz)
Prep 10 mins +
  overnight steeping
Cook 1 hour 10 mins

1 kg (2 lb 4 oz) Seville oranges
2 litres (70 fl oz/8 cups) dry
  Somerset scrumpy
2 kg (4 lb 8 oz/8⅔ cups)
  caster (superfine) sugar

Prepare and sterilise 8 jars (page 27).

Carefully remove the peel of the oranges with a sharp knife, removing the pith. Slice the peel into thin strips. Add to a large preserving pan.

Squeeze the juice from the oranges into the preserving pan and tie the pulp in a piece of muslin (cheesecloth).

Add the cider to the preserving pan with the peel and juice and drop the muslin into the pan too. Leave everything to steep overnight. This will release the pectin and help the marmalade set at the end.

Next day, put the pan over a high heat and bring the juice and cider to the boil. You need to get the liquid very hot and boiling vigorously. Reduce the heat to a simmer for 1 hour. Remove the muslin bag and squeeze any excess juice back into the pan.

Add the sugar to the pan and bring back to the boil. Use a slotted spoon to remove any foam or scum from the top of the marmalade as it cooks.

Boil until the marmalade reaches 105°C (220°F) on a sugar thermometer or test to see if the marmalade will set by popping a teaspoonful onto a cool plate and seeing if it crinkles as it cools. If not, continue heating for another few minutes.

Transfer the marmalade into the prepared jars, seal and label. Store in a cool, dry place until opened, then keep in the refrigerator. It will keep for up to 3 months unopened.

Apple, rhubarb
and ginger jam (118)

Apple and
mint jelly (120)

Crab apple and
blackberry jam (119)

Somerset cider
marmalade (121)

Apple membrillo

Membrillo is traditionally made using quinces, which is why it is also commonly known as quince jelly, but apples work just as well and offer a slightly different take on this delicious accompaniment to a cheese board or ploughman's lunch. You rely on the pectin in the apples to help set the jelly so don't worry about peeling or removing the cores of the apples as this is where most of it is stored.

Makes about 1 kg (2 lb 4 oz)
Prep 10 mins +
    overnight chilling
Cook 1 hour 25 mins

2 kg (4 lb 8 oz) cooking apples,
    such as Bramleys, chopped
300 ml (10 fl oz/
    1¼ cups) water
caster (superfine) sugar,
    equal to half the weight
    of the purée

Line two 23 cm (9 in) square baking pans with baking parchment.

Put the apples and water in a large, heavy-based pan so that the water just covers the fruit. Bring to the boil, then reduce the heat and simmer for about 25 minutes until the apples are soft. Remove from the heat and leave to cool.

Rub the apples through a sturdy sieve (strainer), squashing the apple through the sieve to turn it into a thick purée. Measure the amount of purée you have, and then measure out half as much sugar.

Return the apple purée to the pan along with the sugar. Heat until the apple purée and sugar start to simmer and bubble. Continuously stir for about 1 hour while the purée reduces to about two-thirds of its original volume and becomes thick. Transfer to the prepared containers and leave to cool overnight.

Next morning you should have a thick jelly, which can either be sealed and stored in the refrigerator until needed or cut up and enjoyed right away. It will keep for up to 2 months.

Pickled spiced crab apples

Crab apples are very versatile; they are great in chutney or apple sauce, and can be added to tarts and jams and jellies. They are also delicious pickled and served with cold meats in place of pickled onions.

Makes about 1 kg (2 lb 4 oz)
Prep 10 mins
Cook 20 mins

2 cinnamon sticks
20 cloves
1 whole nutmeg
1 cm (½ in) piece of ginger
   root, sliced
700 ml (24 fl oz/scant
   3 cups) shop-bought or
   homemade Apple cider
   vinegar (page 133)
700 ml (24 fl oz/scant
   3 cups) water
450 g (1 lb/2 cups) caster
   (superfine) sugar
1 kg (2 lb 4 oz) crab apples

Prepare and sterilise 5 or 6 jars (page 27).

Wrap the cinnamon sticks, cloves, nutmeg and ginger in a small piece of muslin (cheesecloth) to create a spice bag. Tie with some kitchen string to secure.

Put the cider vinegar, water and sugar in a large, heavy-based saucepan over a medium heat and stir until the has sugar dissolved. Add the spice bag to the pan, turn up the heat and bring to the boil. Boil for 5 minutes.

While this is cooking, clean the crab apples and trim off black marks or bits left from the stalk or blossom base, then prick the crab apples with a cocktail stick (this will prevent them from breaking up while cooking).

Reduce the pickling juice to a very light simmer. Add the crab apples and allow to simmer for 3–4 minutes. Keep an eye on them as you don't want them to overcook or break up. They need to just start to soften. If they start to break up, reduce the heat, or take them off the heat all together.

Remove the apples from the liquid using a slotted spoon and divide among the prepared jars. Remove the spice bag from the liquid and pour the liquid into the jars, seal and label. Store in a cool, dry place. It will keep for up to 2 months.

Apple and vanilla compôte

This is a slightly different take on a traditional apple sauce recipe. By adding butter and vanilla, it transforms this much-loved classic into the perfect accompaniment for some granola and yoghurt for breakfast, or to be served as a side for dessert.

Serves 4
Prep 10 mins
Cook 10 mins

75 g (2½ oz) unsalted butter
100 g (3½ oz/scant ½ cup)
  caster (superfine) sugar
750 g (1 lb 10 oz) cooking
  apples, such as Bramleys,
  peeled, cored and chopped
½ vanilla pod (bean),
  cut in half lengthways
  and seeds scraped out
pinch of salt

Melt the butter in a saucepan over a medium heat. Add the sugar and cook for a couple minutes until the sugar has dissolved.

Add the chopped apples and reduce the temperature to simmer gently for about 5 minutes until the apples are cooked and start to break down. Make sure that there are still chunks of apple in the sauce for texture. Add the vanilla pod and seeds and a pinch of salt, then stew for a further minute.

Remove the pan from the heat, discard the vanilla pod, and pour the apple into a serving dish. Serve either hot or cold. It will keep in the refrigerator for up to 3 days.

Ultimate apple sauce

Apple sauce is one of the easiest things to make, incredibly simple and a superstar companion to pork, elevating the dish and adding a refreshing new dynamic to a meal. There was really no improving on a traditional recipe, but I have included it within this occasion because, quite frankly, I couldn't write a book on apples without it being in here somewhere. Whether, you're spreading this delicious sweet and sharp accompaniment on roast pork or serving it with some chops, it is sublime in both its flavour and simplicity. What's more, you can easily prepare a large batch and freeze it in small portions for even more convenience. If you would like to mix things up with the sauce, then add some orange zest or lemon zest for added flavour.

Serves 4–6
Prep 5 mins
Cook 10 mins

4 large cooking apples, such as Bramleys, peeled, cored and chopped
75 g (2½ oz/⅓ cup) caster (superfine) sugar
2 tablespoons water
10 g (¼ oz) butter

Put the apples, sugar and water in a saucepan and cook over a medium heat for about 10 minutes, stirring every minute or so, until the sugar dissolves and the apples break down without sticking to the bottom of the pan. (I like to have some chunks of apple in the sauce so don't worry if they aren't completely mashed).

Add the butter and stir to melt through before serving. It will keep in the refrigerator for up to 3 days.

Apple and chilli jelly

Apple and chilli jelly is sweet yet spicy and delicious served with cold meats and cheese. When preparing the apples, chop them up but leave the core and peel on. This is where the most pectin is and will help give you a nicely set jelly.

Makes about 2–2.5 kg
   (4 lb 8 oz–5 lb 10 oz)
Prep 10 mins +
   overnight straining
Cook 30 mins

2 kg (4 lb 8 oz) cooking
   apples, such as Bramleys,
   peeled and chopped
15 g (½ oz) chilli (hot pepper)
   flakes or 5 chopped bird's
   eye chillies
100 ml (3½ fl oz/scant
   ½ cup) shop-bought
   or homemade Apple cider
   vinegar (page 133)
caster (superfine) sugar,
   equal to half the weight
   of the juice

Prepare and sterilise 6 jars (page 27).

Put the apples and chillies in a large, heavy-based saucepan. Add just enough water to cover the apples and bring to the boil. Reduce to a simmer and cook for about 10 minutes until the apples break down.

Add the cider vinegar and bring back to the boil for 2 minutes. Remove from the heat.

Spoon the apple into a fine-mesh strainer lined with muslin (cheesecloth) and let the juice drip into a bowl. This might take a while but don't be tempted to push it through to speed up the process. Let it take its time as this is how you get lovely clear jelly. Ideally, leave the apple dripping overnight.

When all the juice has dripped out, measure the amount of juice you have, and then measure half as much sugar. Then, return the juice to the clean saucepan and add the sugar. Bring to the boil until the sugar has dissolved. Then continue to boil for about 15 minutes until the jelly reaches 105°C (220°F) on a sugar thermometer.

Once it reaches the desired heat, remove from the heat and decant into the prepared jars, seal and label. The jelly will keep for 1 year unopened.

Somerset apple chutney (115)   Apple and tomato relish (112)

Cider-glazed ham (98)   Apple and chilli jelly (129)   Apple crisps (111)

Crab apple and rosemary jelly

Crab apples are great in jellies and jams due to the high pectin levels, and the sweet but sharp flavour combined with the fragrant rosemary makes for an interesting and tasty combination. This is ideal with cold meats or melted in gravies or reductions.

Makes about 2–2.5 kg
(4 lb 8 oz–5 lb 10 oz)
Prep 10 mins +
overnight straining
Cook 30 mins

2 kg (4 lb 8 oz) whole
crab apples, stalks and
blossom removed
50 g (2 oz) sprig of rosemary
100 ml (3½ fl oz/scant
½ cup) shop-bought
or homemade Apple cider
vinegar (page 133)
caster (superfine) sugar,
equal to half the weight
of the juice

Prepare and sterilise 8 jars (page 27).

Put the apples and rosemary in a large, heavy-based saucepan. Add just enough water to cover the apples and bring to a boil. Reduce the heat and simmer for about 10 minutes until the apples break down.

Add the cider vinegar and bring back to the boil for 2 minutes. Remove from the heat.

Spoon the apple into a sieve (strainer) lined with muslin (cheesecloth) and let the juice drip into a bowl. This might take a while but don't be tempted to push it through to speed up the process. Let it take its time as this is how you get lovely clear jelly. Ideally, leave the apple dripping overnight.

When all the juice has dripped out, measure the amount of liquid you have, and then measure out half as much sugar. Then, return the juice to the clean saucepan and add the sugar. Heat gently until the sugar has dissolved, then bring to the boil and continue to boil for about 15 minutes until the jelly reaches 105°C (220°F) on a sugar thermometer, or a few drops on a cold plate wrinkle when pressed.

Once it reaches the desired heat, remove from the heat. Spoon into the prepared jars, seal and label. The jelly will keep for up to 1 year unopened.

Apple cider vinegar

Cider vinegar has been having a bit of a moment and is very much the in-vogue superfood. While it has health benefits and is great for the gut, it is also a larder essential and useful in so many recipes. Plus, making your own cider vinegar is also a great way of using up the peelings and cores that you would usually discard from preparing other dishes. I like to save all my peelings in a bag in the freezer and when I have enough, make a batch of homemade cider vinegar to use them up. Waste not, want not! What's more, by making your own you ensure that you're reserving the precious 'mother' – the good bacteria that hold those benefits – which is usually stripped out during the pasteurisation of mass-produced cider vinegar. It is also important to use organic apples here to ensure that there is nothing on the skin that can taint the taste of the vinegar at all.

Makes about 750 ml
  (25 fl oz/3 cups)
Prep 20 mins
Fermentation 4 weeks

organic apple peelings
  and cores (enough to fill
  a 1 litre (34 fl oz/4 cup) jar
  to three-quarters full)
2 tablespoons caster
  (superfine) sugar
1 litre (34 fl oz/4 cups)
  mineral water

Prepare and sterilise a Kilner (Mason) jar (page 27).

Put the apple bits in the jar so that it is at least three-quarters full, then add the sugar and fill the jar with enough mineral water to cover the apples and fill the jar.

Weigh the apples down using a fermentation weight or small glass jar. You need to make sure the apple pieces are submerged in the water and not poking out. This avoids the apple going mouldy.

Cover the jar with muslin (cheesecloth) and secure with an elastic band. Do not secure the lid.

Leave to ferment in a dark, dry place. A kitchen cupboard away from the oven area will be fine. Store for 4 weeks, checking every few days that there isn't any mould or scum on the surface from any apple that has floated to the top. If there is, remove with a spoon.

After 4 weeks, strain the vinegar to discard the apple pieces and pour the liquid through a muslin back into the jar and secure the lid. Sediment will start to form after a couple of months, but it will keep for up to 1 year.

Sweet Things

The scent, sweetness and texture of apples seems to evoke a wonderful nostalgia among many people. Whether in cakes or crumbles people seem to get rather giddy with excitement at the prospect of tucking into a gooey, appley sweet treat. I could have included many more recipes here as there are endless ways to serve apples for pudding, but this is a selection of some of my favourites. Get the custard at the ready!

Ultimate apple crumble

Crumble is a serious business in my home. If you're like me and, as winter approaches, long for hearty, nutritious, tried-and-tested recipes that never fail to provide you with a winter warming pick-up, then this one is sure to join the fold and sit alongside those other winter essentials, likes stews, puddings and soups.

I also must admit that I got slightly obsessed with creating the perfect crumble recipe when I was younger – testing different apple varieties, alternative ways of cooking the crumble as well as the different spices and ingredient additions you can make. The result? Firstly, to my mind there is only one apple variety that anybody should consider for a crumble. Yes, it might sound lazy or a cliché even, but the Bramley really is the king of the crumble. And a mostly traditional mix of flour, caster (superfine) sugar, butter and a pinch of cinnamon has been constantly and consistently the favoured crumble topping. I like my crumble nice and crunchy, so add some porridge oats and walnuts or hazelnuts as well as pre-cooking the crumble to get it just right. But this is personal preference, and both processes can easily be skipped. The crumble is a hero of a dish that never fails to be an absolute hit at dinner parties, Sunday lunches or even a midweek indulgence.

Serves 6–8
Prep 15 mins
Cook 55 mins

4 large cooking apples, such
  as Bramleys, peeled, cored
  and diced
1½ teaspoons
  ground cinnamon
50 g (5 oz) butter,
  at room temperature
250 g (9 oz/heaped 1 cup)
  caster (superfine) sugar
200 g (7 oz/1⅔ cups) plain
  (all-purpose) flour
50 g (2 oz/½ cup) porridge oats
50 g (2 oz/½ cup) walnuts and/
  or hazelnuts, chopped
1½ tablespoons demerara sugar

To serve
custard (page 138) or vanilla
  ice cream

Preheat a fan oven to 160°C (320°F/gas 4) and line a baking sheet with baking parchment.

Place the diced apples in an ovenproof dish, sprinkle with half the ground cinnamon and a couple dollops of the butter.

Put the sugar, flour and the remaining butter into a large bowl and mix together with your fingertips. You should combine the ingredients by rubbing between your fingers and thumbs to create a breadcrumb-like texture. Then add the oats, walnuts or hazelnuts, sprinkle in the remaining ground cinnamon and mix thoroughly.

Once the dry mix is combined, spread it out evenly on the prepared baking sheet and bake it in the oven for 10 minutes. (This part is optional, but I love doing this to create a particularly crunchy crumble topping.)

Spread the topping over the apples and sprinkle the demerara sugar over the top. Then, cook in the oven for 45 minutes until golden brown and bubbling round the edges.

Serve with a healthy dollop of custard or vanilla ice cream. Or simply with a big bowl and spoon.

Salted caramel baked apples

The salted caramel centre of these apples oozes out, almost seductively, onto the plate when you cut into them with your knife. These mini volcano-like apples are a delicious, fun and naughty but seriously nice treat served with vanilla ice cream or cream.

Serves 4
Prep 10 mins
Cook 25 mins

4 large sweet, sharp eating
   (dessert) apples, such as
   Granny Smith or Red Falstaff
50 g (2 oz/½ cup) pecans
   or walnuts
25 g (1 oz/scant ¼ cup)
   pumpkin seeds
½ teaspoon ground cinnamon
2 tablespoons runny honey
¼ teaspoon sea salt
cream or vanilla ice cream,
   to serve

For the salted caramel
75 g (2½ oz) butter
3 tablespoons soft light
   brown sugar
½ teaspoon sea salt
2 tablespoons double
   (heavy) cream

Preheat a fan oven to 200°C (400°F/gas 8) and line a baking sheet with baking parchment.

Use a corer or small, sharp knife to remove the core of the apples so that you have a whole apple without the middle. Next, take some more baking parchment and cut it into four squares large enough to wrap around the apples. Wrap the apples with the paper and tie the paper packages closed with some kitchen string – not too tight as you want the steam to escape while cooking.

Stand the apple packages upright on the baking sheet and bake for 10 minutes until the apples are just tender but still holding their shape.

Meanwhile, put the nuts and seeds in a saucepan and toast over a medium heat for 3–4 minutes until lightly browned and fragrant, tossing constantly to make sure they don't burn. Then add the ground cinnamon and toast for a further 30 seconds before adding the honey. Let the honey bubble around the nuts and seeds and add the sea salt. Stir everything together and then turn out onto a plate lined with baking parchment to cool and harden. Once hardened, roughly chop into pieces.

To make the salted caramel sauce, melt the butter in a saucepan and add the sugar. Stir in well and keep stirring while the sugar dissolves, being careful not to let it burn. Add the sea salt and finally the cream. You'll be left with a smooth, light caramel.

When the apples are done, remove them from the oven, remove the string and open the packages slightly. Spoon some of the caramel into each of the spaces in the middle of the apples, filling the core of the apples with the sauce, stopping before it spills over the sides.

Lastly top the apples with the nuts and seeds and return to the oven to bake for a further 5 minutes before serving with a drizzle of cream or vanilla ice cream.

Poached apples in cider brandy sauce

Poached apples make a perfect dessert, served warm with some ice cream, and they are also equally delicious served with breakfast alongside some yoghurt and granola – just leave out the brandy when making the sauce. This recipe spices them with cinnamon but you can experiment with the spices and flavourings depending on what you'd like to serve them with – vanilla and ginger also work really well.

Serves 4
Prep 10 mins
Cook 35 mins

600 ml (20 fl oz/2½ cups) medium sweet cider
2 tablespoons runny honey, preferably Somerset
1 cinnamon stick
4 sharp, eating (dessert) apples, such as Granny Smith James Grieve, Fiesta or Cox's, peeled and cored
2 tablespoons Somerset cider brandy

To serve
vanilla ice cream

Heat the cider in a saucepan until simmering. Add the honey and the cinnamon stick and stir until the honey has dissolved.

Carefully add the apples and simmer for 20–25 minutes until soft but still holding their shape. Once the apples are cooked, take them out and put to one side.

Add the Somerset cider brandy to the saucepan and bring to the boil. Continue boiling until the liquid has reduced by half.

Serve the apples with a generous spoonful of the sauce and some vanilla ice cream.

All-American apple pie

A book all about apples wouldn't be complete without the king of the apple desserts: the apple pie! While writing this book, when I talked to people about their favourite apple recipes, the apple pie was a regular, firm favourite and something that everybody had an opinion on. What made the best pie? Which were the best apples to use? And so on.

Despite the title of this recipe, I am not seriously proclaiming that this is the ultimate American-style apple pie – I wouldn't dare. However, I wanted to include the best, most authentic and tasty apple pie recipe I could. So, I thought the best place to go and find it was the country that it is most famous for making it. The good old USA.

I travelled to the States on the hunt for perfect pie and on this trip, I learned two things. One, Americans take apple pie incredibly seriously (you could even refer to it as a religion); and two, the key to the best pie recipes are a very closely guarded secret, something that is passed down from generation to generation. Everybody has their preferred method, and treasured memories of being served fresh, warm apple pie as a child by their mothers and grandmothers.

But were they willing to share their most fiercely guarded secrets? Not really, no. However, I did glean some insight from my trip, most notably adding ground hazelnuts and cinnamon to the pastry and also mixing up the apple varieties in the filling. I've played around with the recipe and apple mixtures here and I think I've found something that is the perfect mix between sweet and sharp and then the textures of the soft, gooey, appley sauce filling and sturdier chunks of apple that helps hold the pie up.

RECIPE METHOD OVERLEAF ⟶

Serves 6–8

Prep 30–40 mins + chilling
  and standing

Cook 50 mins

For the pastry

475 g (1 lb 1 oz/3¾ cups) plain
  (all-purpose) flour, plus
  extra for dusting

100 g (3½ oz/heaped ¾ cup)
  icing (confectioner's) sugar

1 teaspoon ground cinnamon

50 g (2 oz/scant ½ cup) finely
  ground hazelnuts

250 g (9 oz) butter, cold and
  cut into small cubes

2 eggs, beaten

1 tablespoon whole milk

granulated sugar, to sprinkle

For the filling

175 g (6 oz/⅓ cup) caster
  (superfine) sugar

1 teaspoon ground cinnamon

¼ teaspoon allspice

pinch of salt

juice of ½ lemon

1 sharp, green eating
  (dessert) apple, such
  as Granny Smith, peeled,
  cored and sliced

1 sweet eating (dessert)
  apple, such as Gala, peeled,
  cored and sliced

2 cooking apples, such
  as Bramleys, peeled,
  cored and sliced

a few drops of vanilla extract

To serve

custard or vanilla ice cream

To make the pastry, sift the flour, icing sugar and ground cinnamon into a large bowl. Rub the ground hazelnuts and cubed butter into the flour and sugar with your hands until you get a crumble-like mixture.

Add the eggs and carefully work in with your hands until you have a dough, gradually adding the milk to get the right consistency that is firm and not too sticky. Be careful not to mix it too much – you don't want to overwork the pastry. Flour the dough lightly and wrap it in cling film (plastic wrap) before popping it in the refrigerator for 30 minutes.

To make the filling, mix the sugar, cinnamon, allspice and salt in a bowl. Add the lemon juice and sliced apples and toss in the sugar mixture until well coated. Stir in the vanilla extract.

To assemble the pie, take the pastry out of the refrigerator and let it stand for 30 minutes. Preheat a fan oven to 180°C (350°F/gas 6) and grease a 23 cm (9 in) pie dish with butter.

Flour a clean work surface and cut the pastry in half. Roll out one half large enough to cover the bottom and sides of the prepared dish. Place the pastry in the dish and prick the bottom with a fork. Place in the freezer for 10 minutes while you prepare the pastry lid or lattice top.

For a plain lid, simply roll out the second piece of pastry to slightly larger than the dish.

To create a lattice, roll out the pastry for the lid on a floured surface so that it about 2.5 cm (1 in) larger than the actual pie dish. Cut the pastry into 1 cm (½ in) ribbons. I find a pizza cutter is the most accurate and easiest tool to use.

Take the pastry base out of the freezer and fill with the apple, sugar and spice mix.

To make the plain pie, moisten the edges of the pastry and cover the pie base with the top, sealing and crimping the edges together.

For a latticed top, lay four or five strips of pastry parallel on top of the pie about 2 cm (¾ in) apart. Fold back every other strip halfway. Place the pie so that the strips are vertical in front of you. Place one strip of dough horizontally across the middle of the pie at right angles to the other strips. Unfold the folded strips.

Fold back the vertical strips that are under the single strip. Add another horizontal strip below the first one, then unfold the folded strips. Continue until the bottom half of the pie is covered, then repeat with other half.

Moisten and seal the edges, then trim off any excess pastry. Brush the pastry with the beaten egg and sprinkle with a couple of pinches of granulated sugar.

Bake in the oven for 50 minutes, or until the pie is golden, and serve warm with a healthy dollop of custard or vanilla ice cream.

Autumn fruit pavlova with apple and vanilla cream

Pavlova is always a popular treat. I like the fact that you can mix and match the fruit depending on what's readily available. Heading out into the orchard or on a country walk and picking blackberries to add to the pavlova makes a lovely addition, for example. You could also use pears, plums, cherries, figs... just try it with your favourites.

Serves 12
Prep 35 mins + cooling
Cook 45 mins

For the apple and vanilla cream
1 large cooking apple,
 such as a Bramley, peeled,
 cored and chopped
4 tablespoons caster
 (superfine) sugar
2 tablespoons water
½ vanilla pod (bean), split
 in half lengthways and
 seeds scraped out
400 ml (13 fl oz/
 generous 1½ cups)
 double (heavy) cream
zest of ½ lime

For the meringue
6 egg whites
1 tablespoon white
 wine vinegar
350 g (12 oz/1½ cups) caster
 (superfine) sugar

For the topping
selection of autumn fruits:
 apples, blackberries, pears,
 plums, figs, pomegranates
juice of ½ lemon

To serve
mint, finely sliced
lime zest

To make the apple and vanilla cream, heat the apple, half of the sugar and the water in a pan over a medium heat. Stir until the apple begins to break down, then simmer for 5 minutes until you have a smooth apple sauce. Stir in the vanilla seeds and leave to one side to fully cool.

Whisk the cream and the remaining sugar in an electric mixer until you have stiff peaks. This will take about 5 minutes. Add the lime zest and mix through.

Once the apple sauce is fully cool, lightly stir through the cream. You don't want to mix it completely; it should have a marbled effect.

To make the meringue, preheat a fan oven to 120°C (250°F/gas 1) and cut three pieces of baking parchment to fit three baking sheets. Draw a 20 cm (8 in) circle clearly onto each piece of parchment, then turn the paper upside down on the baking sheet; you should still be able to see the circles.

Now make the meringue. Using an electric mixer with the whisk attachment, beat the egg whites and vinegar on a medium-high speed for a couple minutes. Add the sugar, one tablespoon at a time, and continue beating until you have very stiff peaks. Using a spatula divide the meringue between the three circles and use the back of the spatula to spread the meringue into even discs that fill the circles.

Bake in the oven for 40 minutes until firm. Turn the oven off and leave the oven door ajar to allow the meringues to cool and harden in the oven. This will take about 1 hour 30 minutes.

To assemble the pavlova, slice and prepare your chosen fruit. For the apples, slice with the skins on and soak in some cool water with the lemon juice for a few minutes so that they keep their colour. Drain before adding to the other fruit.

Just before serving, place one meringue disc on a cake stand and spread a third of the apple cream on top. Then add a third of the fruit.

Top with the next meringue disc, spread a third of the cream and another third of the fruit. Finally repeat with the last of the ingredients. Garnish with mint and lime zest, then serve.

Apple and almond tart with cider brandy cream

The flavours of almond and brandy complement each other deliciously in this tart.

Serves 8
Prep 35 mins + chilling
Cook 1 hour

For the pastry
475 g (1 lb 1 oz/3¾ cups) plain
   (all-purpose) flour, plus
   extra for dusting
100 g (3½ oz/heaped ¾ cup)
   icing (confectioner's) sugar
50 g (2 oz) finely
   ground hazelnuts
250 g (9 oz) butter, cold
   and cut into small cubes
2 eggs, beaten
1 tablespoon whole milk

For the filling
100 g (3½ oz) butter
100 g (3½ oz/heaped ¾ cup)
   icing (confectioner's) sugar
2 eggs, beaten
100 g (3½ oz/1 cup)
   ground almonds
zest of ½ lemon
4 crisp, sweet eating (dessert)
   apples, such as Fiesta
   or Jazz, peeled, cored and
   thinly sliced into rounds
1 tablespoon demerara sugar

For the cider brandy cream
150 ml (5 fl oz/scant ⅔ cup)
   double (heavy) cream
25 g (1 oz/2 tablespoons)
   caster (superfine) sugar
2 tablespoons Somerset cider
   brandy or Calvados

To make the pastry, sift the flour and icing sugar into a large mixing bowl. Add the ground hazelnuts and butter and rub them into the flour and sugar with your fingertips until you get a crumble-like mixture.

Add the eggs and milk and carefully work in with your hands until you have a dough. Be careful not to mix it too much – you don't want to overwork the pastry. Cut the dough in half, lightly flour and wrap the two pieces in cling film (plastic wrap) before popping in the refrigerator for 1 hour.

To make the filling, cream together the butter and icing sugar in a large mixing bowl until light and fluffy. Slowly add the beaten eggs a little at a time, mixing well between each addition. Gently fold in the almonds and lemon zest until combined. Leave to one side.

To make the cider brandy cream, whisk the cream and sugar together until you get soft peaks. Slowly add the cider brandy, whisking well in between each addition. Refrigerate until ready to serve.

To assemble and bake, take one half of the pastry out of the refrigerator 30 minutes before you need it. (The other half of pastry can be reserved for another recipe.) Preheat a fan oven to 160°C (320°F/gas 4) and grease a 23 cm (9 in) springform tart dish with butter.

Flour a smooth work surface. Roll out the pastry large enough to cover the bottom and sides of the tart dish. Place the pastry in the dish, then push into the edges with your thumbs. Prick the bottom with a fork and trim the edges off and then pop in the freezer for 10 minutes before filling.

Remove the pastry from the freezer, fill with the almond filling, arrange the apple rounds on top and sprinkle over the demerara sugar. Bake in the oven for 1 hour until the apples are golden brown and the centre is cooked. Leave to cool for at least 15 minutes before serving to allow the frangipane to firm up.

Serve warm with a dollop of the cider brandy cream.

Apple and date pancakes

Thick American-style pancakes with chunky sweet and tangy apple sauce, served with vanilla ice cream for extra indulgence.

Makes 12
Prep 10 mins
Cook 30 mins

For the pancake batter
50 g (2 oz/1¼ cups) plain
   (all-purpose) flour
2 teaspoons ground cinnamon
1 teaspoons baking powder
2 eggs, beaten
450 ml (15¾ fl oz/scant
   2 cups) whole milk
30 g (1 oz/scant ¼ cup)
   dates, pitted and very
   finely chopped
small knob of butter,
   for cooking

For the filling
30 g (1 oz) butter
600 g (1 lb 5 oz) cooking
   apples, such as Bramleys,
   peeled, cored and sliced
80 g (3 oz/⅓ cup) caster
   (superfine) sugar
juice of ½ lemon

To serve
maple syrup
vanilla ice cream

First make the pancake batter. Sift the flour, cinnamon and baking powder into a mixing bowl and make a well in the middle. Add the eggs and mix with a fork to combine. Gradually add the milk, mixing well as you do, until you have a smooth batter. Stir in the dates and refrigerate until you're ready to cook the pancakes.

To make the filling, melt the butter in a saucepan over a medium heat. Add the apple slices, sugar and lemon juice. Cook for about 10 minutes until the sugar has dissolved and the apple has cooked, but not broken down completely. The idea is to have nice chunks of apple in the sauce.

When you're ready to cook, heat a 20 cm (8 in) non-stick pan or frying pan (skillet) over a medium heat. Melt the butter in the pan, then add about half a ladle of batter. Tilt the pan to spread the batter over the base of the pan and fry for several minutes until nicely golden on each side. Keep the pancakes you have made warm while you make the remaining pancakes.

When ready to serve, fill the pancakes with the apple filling, roll them up and serve with a drizzle of maple syrup and some vanilla ice cream.

Rose de pommes tart

This tart is always a show-stopper, especially if you can take the time to make the dainty apple roses. I will be honest, it does take a while to do, but it is worth it. If you're tight on time, then sliced apple on top works just as well. Just skip the apple roses section, slice the apple into eighths after coring, leaving the skin on, and fan them out on top of the custard.

Serves 6–8
Prep 50 mins + chilling
Cook 30 mins

For the pastry
250 g (9 oz/2 cups) plain (all-purpose) flour, plus extra for dusting
50 g (2 oz/heaped ⅓ cup) icing (confectioner's) sugar
grated zest of ½ lemon
125 g (4 oz) butter, cold and cut into small cubes
1 egg, beaten
½ tablespoon whole milk

For the custard
500 ml (17 fl oz/2 cups) whole milk
½ vanilla pod (bean), halved and seeds scraped out
4 eggs
160 g (5½ oz/scant ¾ cup) caster (superfine) sugar
4 tablespoons plain (all-purpose) flour

For the filling
4 tablespoons strawberry jam (jelly)
110 g (3¾ oz) butter, at room temperature
100 g (3½ oz/scant ½ cup) caster (superfine) sugar
juice of 2 lemons
500 g (1 lb 2 oz) Gala or red eating (dessert) apples
1 tablespoon soft light brown sugar

To make the pastry, sift the flour and icing sugar into a large mixing bowl. Add the lemon zest and cubed butter and rub them into the flour and sugar with your fingertips until you get a crumble-like mixture.

Add the egg and milk. Carefully work in with your hands until you have a dough, but don't want to overwork the pastry. Flour the dough lightly and cut in half. Wrap in cling film (plastic wrap) before popping it in the refrigerator for 30 minutes.

To make the custard, put the milk and vanilla pod and seeds in a heavy-based saucepan and bring to the boil over a medium heat.

In a separate bowl, whisk the eggs and sugar together to form a thick paste. Stir in the flour until combined.

Remove the vanilla pod from the milk and very slowly and gradually pour the hot milk over the egg mixture, whisking continuously.

Pour the mixture back into the saucepan and heat very gently over a low heat until the custard thickens, stirring all the time. Lay a piece of cling film (plastic wrap) touching the surface of the custard to avoid a skin forming. Set to one side.

Take a pastry half out of the refrigerator and leave to come to room temperature. (Use the other half in another recipe.) Preheat a fan oven to 180°C (350°F/gas 6) and grease a 23 cm (9 in) tart dish with butter.

Roll out the pastry on a lightly floured surface. Press into a tart dish and prick the base with a fork. Blind bake in the oven for 20 minutes until it is golden. While the pastry is still hot, spread the strawberry jam onto the base.

For the rest of the filling, put the butter and sugar in a saucepan and heat gently until the butter has melted and the sugar dissolved. Do not let the mixture boil. Leave to cool to room temperature.

Pour the lemon juice into a large bowl and stir in the melted butter and sugar. Cut the apples in half, then core and slice them as thinly as possible using a mandolin and add the slices to the bowl. Ensure the apple is covered with the liquid and leave to stand for 15 minutes. This will 'cook' the apples and make them more pliable to shape.

Pour the custard into the tart base so it comes halfway up the side. Then, take one slice of apple at a time and roll one around another. You'll need about four or five slices to create a rose. Cut the base of the rose flat and place into the custard to hold it in place. Repeat until your tart is full of apple roses.

Preheat a fan oven to 160°C (320°F/gas 4). Sprinkle the tart with brown sugar and bake for 20 minutes before serving nice and warm.

Apple flapjacks

An easy and tasty treat to grab on the go, these apple flapjacks have a gooey apple sauce centre that starts to melt into the oats, making them deliciously soft in the middle.

Makes 18
Prep 10 mins
Cook 35 mins

2 cooking apples, such
    as Bramleys, cored
    and chopped
1 tablespoon water
175 g (6 oz) butter
150 ml (5 fl oz/scant
    ⅔ cup) runny honey
400 g (14 oz/4 cups)
    rolled oats
2 tablespoons pumpkin seeds
1 teaspoon ground cinnamon
1 teaspoon ground ginger
100 g (3½ oz/scant ¾ cup)
    sultanas (golden raisins)
2 crisp, sweet eating (dessert)
    apples, such as Cox's
    or Fiesta, peeled, cored
    and finely chopped
sweet apple slices,
    to decorate

Preheat a fan oven to 180°C (350°F/gas 6) and grease a deep 30 cm x 23 cm (12 in x 9 in) baking dish with butter.

Put the apples and water in a saucepan and bring to a simmer over a medium heat. Continue to simmer gently until the apples start to break down into an apple sauce consistency. Remove from the heat and set to one side to cool.

Next, melt the butter in a separate pan. Add the honey and stir together for a minute to melt together.

In a large mixing bowl, add the oats, pumpkin seeds, ground cinnamon, ground ginger, sultanas and the eating apples. Mix together. Pour the butter and honey over the oat mixture and stir until all the oat mixture is coated.

Pour half the mixture into the prepared baking dish and flatten down well with the back of a spoon, ensuring you get right into the edges.

Pour the Bramley apple sauce over the mixture in the dish so that it covers the flapjack mix. Then pour the rest of the oat mixture on top and flatten with a spoon. Top with the extra apple slices.

Bake in the oven for 25 minutes until golden brown and starting to darken at the edges. Remove from the oven and leave to cool for a few minutes, then mark into squares while still warm. Leave in the dish to cool completely before turning out on a rack.

Chop into squares and serve.

Apple crumble muffins

Tasty spiced apple muffins topped with apple crumble topping – a mischievous but truly delicious afternoon treat.

Makes 8
Prep 20 mins
Cook 25 mins

For the muffins
50 g (2 oz/1¼ cups) plain
   (all-purpose) flour
100 g (3½ oz/scant ½ cup)
   caster (superfine) sugar
1½ teaspoons baking powder
2 teaspoons ground cinnamon
½ teaspoon freshly
   grated nutmeg
pinch of salt
1 sweet, juicy eating (dessert)
   apple, such as Cox's, cored
   and grated (shredded)
120 ml (4 fl oz/½ cup)
   whole milk
1 egg, beaten
4 tablespoons vegetable oil

For the crumble
50 g (2 oz/½ cup) rolled oats
40 g (1½ oz) butter,
   at room temperature
½ teaspoon
   ground cinnamon
25 g (1 oz/2 tablespoons)
   demerara sugar

Preheat a fan oven to 170°C (340°F/gas 5) and grease an 8-hole muffin tin with butter or oil, or line with paper muffin cases.

Mix the flour, sugar, baking powder, cinnamon, nutmeg and pinch of salt in a large mixing bowl. Once combined well, add the grated apple.

Combine the milk, beaten egg and vegetable oil together and gradually add to the bowl, mixing all the time. Once everything is combined, spoon equally into the prepared tin.

Next, in a bowl, mix the oats for the crumble with the soft butter, cinnamon and sugar together until well combined. Top each muffin with a spoonful of the crumble mix.

Bake the muffins in the oven for 25 minutes until brown and crunchy on top. Leave on a wire rack to cool. They will keep in an airtight container for up to 3 days.

Apple and cinnamon swirls

Danish pastries are full of appley goodness and my favourite by a long shot is the cinnamon swirl. There's something completely satisfying about the warming spicy mixture and soft fruit encased in golden crispy pastry and topped with icing sugar. My perfect breakfast treat served with a strong coffee. Save the citrus juices for another recipe.

Makes 24
Prep 20 mins
Cook 20 mins

2 x 320 g (10¾ oz) sheets
  ready-rolled puff pastry
a little flour, for dusting
110 g (3¾ oz) butter,
  at room temperature
125 g (4 oz/⅔ cup) soft dark
  brown sugar
4 teaspoons ground cinnamon
250 g (9 oz) cooking apples,
  such as Bramleys, or eating
  (dessert) apples, such
  as Cox's, cored and
  finely chopped
50 g (2 oz/heaped ⅓ cup)
  sultanas (golden raisins)
zest of ½ orange
zest of 1 lemon
1 teaspoon vanilla extract
1 egg, beaten

For the icing (frosting)
100 g (3½ oz/heaped ¾ cup)
  icing (confectioner's) sugar
1 tablespoon water
a few drops of vanilla extract

Preheat a fan oven to 180°C (350°F/gas 6) and line two large baking sheets with baking parchment.

Lay the pastry sheets on a floured surface.

In a large mixing bowl, combine the butter, soft dark brown sugar, cinnamon, cooking apples, sultanas, orange and lemon zest and vanilla extract. Mix well so that everything is coated.

Leaving a 2.5 cm (1 in) wide strip along one of the longest edges, spread the filling mixture equally over the two sheets of pastry right up to the edges.

Starting at the longest edge, roll each pastry sheet in tight turns so that the filling is completely wrapped in pastry. When you get to the filling-free border, brush with a little of the beaten egg to help seal them.

Using a sharp knife, cut each roll into 12 equal slices, turn them over on their side, on the baking sheet, so that the apple and cinnamon swirl is visible, making sure there is room around each swirl to allow them to spread in the oven.

Brush the swirls with the remainder of the egg and bake for 20 minutes until golden brown and crisp.

While the swirls are baking, make the icing. Mix the icing sugar, water and vanilla extract in a bowl until thick and smooth.

When the swirls are baked, remove from the oven and transfer to a wire rack. When cool, drizzle the icing sugar over the swirls and serve.

I like to think of this cake as containing all the best flavours of the typical English garden. Delicately sweet and fragrant apples and lavender, with the soothing honey and cream cheese icing on top.

Serves 8
Prep 20 mins + cooling
Cook 40 mins

For the cake
125 g (4 oz/1 cup) plain
   (all-purpose) flour
75 g (2½ oz/⅓ cup) caster
   (superfine) sugar
1 teaspoon baking powder
75 g (2½ oz) butter,
   at room temperature
3 eggs, beaten
100 ml (3½ fl oz/scant
   ½ cup) runny honey
2 sprigs of lavender, flowers
   only, or dried cook's lavender
200 g (7 oz) cooking apples,
   such as Bramleys, peeled,
   cored and cut into chunks

*For the honey and lavender
   icing (frosting)*
50 ml (1¾ fl oz/
   3 tablespoons) double
   (heavy) cream
100 g (3½ oz) cream cheese
1 tablespoon runny honey
40 g (1½ oz/⅓ cup) icing
   (confectioner's) sugar
1 sprig of lavender, flowers
   only, or dried cook's
   lavender, plus extra
   for decorating
grated zest of ½ lemon

Preheat a fan oven to 160°C (320°F/gas 4) and grease the base of a round 23 cm (9 in) springform cake pan with butter and line with baking parchment.

Mix the flour, sugar and baking powder together in an electric mixer. Add the butter and mix on a medium speed until smooth. Gradually add the eggs a little at a time, allowing them to be fully mixed in before adding more. Pour in the honey and then add the lavender flowers and mix to combine.

Remove the bowl from the mixer and gently stir in three-quarters of the apple chunks. Pour the mixture into the prepared cake pan, then arrange the remaining apples on top. Bake in the oven for 40 minutes until a skewer inserted in the centre comes out clean.

While the cake is baking, make the icing. Whisk the cream until it forms soft peaks. Add the cream cheese and whisk together. Add the honey and icing sugar and continue whisking until everything is combined. Lastly add the lavender flowers and lemon zest and fold through. Cover and chill in the refrigerator until you're ready to serve.

Leave the cake to cool in the pan for 15 minutes. Once cool enough to handle, turn out on to a wire to finish cooling.

When you're ready to serve, take the icing from the refrigerator and generously swirl it over the top of the cake using the back of a spoon. Serve with a piping hot cup of tea!

Maple and apple upside-down cake

Sweet caramelised apples and light sponge drizzled with a maple sauce makes this upside-down cake a hit when served at home. The texture of apples and the way the sticky, sweet sauce is absorbed by the sponge is a taste sensation and perfect served still warm with some vanilla ice cream.

Serves 8
Prep 15 mins + cooling
Cook 50 mins

For the maple-glazed apples
75 g (2½ oz) butter
100 g (3½ oz/scant ½ cup)
   caster (superfine) sugar
50 ml (1¾ fl oz) maple syrup
½ teaspoon ground cinnamon
4 crisp, sharp eating (dessert)
   apples, such as Granny
   Smith or Blenheim Orange,
   peeled, cored and cut
   into wedges

For the cake
175 g (6 oz) butter
175 g (6 oz/¾ cup) caster
   (superfine) sugar
3 eggs, beaten
1 teaspoon vanilla extract
175 g (6 oz/scant 1½ cups)
   self-raising flour
½ teaspoon bicarbonate
   of soda (baking soda)
¼ teaspoon salt
3 tablespoons whole milk

To serve
vanilla ice cream

Preheat a fan oven to 180°C (350°F/gas 6) and grease the base of a 23 cm (9 in) round cake pan with butter and line with baking parchment.

To make the maple-glazed apples, melt the butter over a medium heat in a large saucepan. Add the sugar and heat until dissolved. Stir in the maple syrup and ground cinnamon, then add the apple slices. Cook the apples for 3 minutes or so until they begin to soften.

Remove from the heat and, when cool enough to handle, arrange the apple slices, slightly overlapping, in a circular decoration around the prepared pan. Pour the glaze over the apples.

Next, make the cake batter. Cream together the butter and sugar in an electric mixer until pale and fluffy. Slowly add the beaten eggs, mixing well between additions. Mix in the vanilla extract.

Sift the flour and bicarbonate of soda together and add the salt. Add a tablespoon to the mixer at a time until everything is well combined.

Next, slowly add the milk to the mix until you have a light and creamy batter.

Turn the batter out onto the apples and smooth flat with the back of a spoon. Bake in the oven for 40 minutes until golden and a knife inserted in the middle comes out clean.

Remove from the oven and leave to stand for 10 minutes, to cool slightly, in the pan, before turning out on to a plate. Serve warm with some vanilla ice cream.

Apple and rosemary cake

The woodiness of the rosemary always brings out the freshness of the apples, and this recipe combines these flavours in a sweet and aromatic cake.

Serves 8
Prep 10 mins
Cook 10 mins

600 g (1 lb 5 oz) cooking
  apples, such as Bramleys,
  peeled, cored and cut
  into chunks
zest and juice of 1 lemon
150 g (5 oz/1¼ cups) plain
  (all-purpose) flour
1 teaspoon baking powder
pinch of salt
150 g (5 oz/⅔ cup) caster
  (superfine) sugar
3 eggs, beaten
110 g (3¾ oz) unsalted
  butter, melted
1 tablespoon finely chopped
  rosemary leaves, plus some
  whole sprigs for garnishing
1 tablespoon flaked
  (slivered) almonds
2 tablespoons apricot
  jam (jelly)
1 teaspoon lemon juice

Preheat a fan oven to 180°C (350°F/gas 6) and grease the base of a 2 lb (900 g) loaf pan with butter and line with baking parchment.

Put the apple chunks in a bowl and toss them in the lemon juice.

Sift the flour and baking powder into a separate mixing bowl with a pinch of salt and the sugar. Gradually add the beaten eggs, whisking well all the time. Add the melted butter, chopped rosemary and lemon zest and mix well to combine.

Drain the apple slices and fold into the cake mix. Then pour the mix into the prepared pan and add the rosemary sprigs and flaked almonds on top.

Bake in the oven for 35 minutes until golden and well risen, and a skewer inserted in the middle comes out clean. Remove from the oven and leave to cool, in the pan, for 10 minutes before turning out onto a wire rack to finish cooling.

While the cake is baking, heat the apricot jam and lemon juice over a low heat until melted down. When the cake is slightly cooled, brush the apricot jam over the top.

Serve when cool.

Apple, raspberry and almond cake

This was the very first cake I made for this cookbook. I wanted to start by creating something that combined some of my favourite flavours: apple (obviously), raspberry, almond and rose. So, essentially, I threw them all together to see what happened. The result is a fragrant and moist sponge filled with fruit. The nature of adding fruit to cake, especially sponge, means that you might find you need a little longer than an hour in the oven. This is fine, just top with foil and let it bake until done.

Serves 8
Prep 15 mins
Cook 1 hour

For the cake
150 g (5 oz/1½ cups)
   ground almonds
250 g (9 oz/heaped 1 cup)
   caster (superfine) sugar
185 g (6½ oz/1½ cups)
   self-raising flour
½ teaspoon baking powder
¼ teaspoon salt
4 eggs, beaten
grated zest of ½ lemon
1–2 drops of rose water
200 g (7 oz) unsalted butter,
   at room temperature
125 g (4 oz) raspberries
2 sharp eating (dessert)
   apples, such as Granny
   Smith or Cox's, peeled,
   cored and diced into
   1 cm (½ in) cubes

For the icing (frosting)
50 g (2 oz/heaped ⅓ cup)
   icing (confectioner's) sugar
¼ teaspoon almond extract

Preheat a fan oven to 160°C (320°F/gas 4) and grease the base of a 23 cm (9 in) springform cake pan with butter and line with baking parchment.

Put the ground almonds, sugar, flour, baking powder and salt in a bowl and mix well. Gradually add the beaten eggs, mixing well all the time.

Add the grated lemon zest and rose water – be careful not to add too much rose water as it is a really intense flavour.

Fold in the butter and mix thoroughly so that everything is well blended. Finally, gently mix in the raspberries and apple, being careful not to mix too much so that the raspberries stay whole.

Pour the mixture into the cake pan and smooth the top of the cake with the back of a spoon to make it level.

Bake in the centre of the oven for 1 hour, keeping a close eye on it so that it doesn't burn on top – you may need to cover with foil for the last 10 minutes. Check the cake is thoroughly cooked and a skewer inserted in the middle comes out clean before removing from the oven. Leave to rest in the pan for 10 minutes before turning out.

While the cake is baking, make the icing. Mix the icing sugar with the almond extract and a drop of cold water until combined into a thick icing. Once the cake is cooled, drizzle with icing, slice, grab a fork and tuck in!

Apple, cardamom and poppy cake

Toasting the cardamom seeds releases their flavour and make this a beautifully scented cake that is ideal with a cup of tea.

Serves 8
Prep 20 mins
Cook 55 mins

6 cardamom pods
125 g (4 oz/1 cup) plain
  (all-purpose) flour
1 teaspoon baking powder
50 g (2 oz) butter,
  at room temperature
110 g (3¾ oz/½ cup)
  caster (superfine) sugar
1 egg, beaten
2 tablespoons whole milk
salt
1 tablespoon poppy seeds
1 cooking apple, such
  as a Bramley, peeled,
  cored and chopped

Preheat a fan oven to 180°C (350°F/gas 6) and grease the base of a 23 cm (9 in) square cake pan with butter and line with baking parchment.

Break open the cardamom pods and remove the seeds. Heat the seeds in a dry pan to toast for 2–3 minutes, making sure they don't brown too much or burn. When toasted, transfer to a grinder or pestle and mortar and grind into a fine powder. Set aside.

Sift the flour and baking powder together into a bowl. Separately, in an electric mixer, cream together the butter and sugar.

Gradually mix in the beaten egg a little at a time. Add the flour and baking powder mixture a spoonful at a time. Then add the milk and a pinch of salt until everything is well blended.

Mix in the poppy seeds and the ground cardamom. Finally, stir in three-quarters of the apple chunks so they are evenly spread through the mixture.

Pour the mixture into the prepared pan and top with the last of the apple chunks. Bake in the oven for 50 minutes until the cake is golden brown and a skewer inserted in the middle comes out clean. Leave to cool in the pan for 5 minutes, then turn out to finish cooling on a wire rack.

Apple, date and coffee loaf

A slightly different take on a traditional coffee cake, this one has a delicious crunchy topping and sticky sweet coffee sauce. Serve it with some ice cream for dessert – warm from the oven – then, if you are lucky, there will be a slice to serve with coffee the following day.

Serves 8
Prep 20 mins
Cook 40–45 mins

For the cake
300 g (10½ oz/1⅓ cups) caster (superfine) sugar
110 g (3¾ oz) butter, melted
3 eggs, beaten
250 g (9 oz/2 cups) plain (all-purpose) flour
2 teaspoons baking powder
1 teaspoon ground cinnamon
½ teaspoon salt
a few drops of vanilla extract
50 g (2 oz/⅓ cup) chopped dates
2 sharp, green eating (dessert) apples, such as Granny Smith, peeled, cored and finely chopped
50 g (2 oz/heaped ¼ cup) soft light brown sugar
100 g (3½ oz/generous ¾ cup) pecans, chopped

For the coffee icing (frosting)
1 teaspoon instant coffee granules
10 g (¼ oz) butter
125 g (4 oz/⅔ cup) soft light brown sugar
2 tablespoons icing (confectioner's) sugar

Preheat a fan oven to 180°C (350°F/gas 6) and line a 30 cm (12 in) square loaf tin with baking parchment.

In an electric mixer, cream together the sugar and melted butter. Gradually add the beaten eggs.

Sift the flour, baking powder and half the cinnamon together, then gradually add to the mixer a little at a time. Add the salt and vanilla extract and mix well. Fold in the dates and apples, then turn the mixture into the prepared pan and level the top.

In a bowl, mix together the light brown sugar and the remaining ground cinnamon and stir in the pecans so that they are roughly coated in the sugar and cinnamon mixture. Sprinkle the sugar pecans over the top of the cake. You may need to cover the cake with foil part way through to prevent the crunchy pecan topping from browning too much or even burning.

Bake in the oven for 40–45 minutes until the cake is turning a deep golden colour on top and a skewer inserted in the middle comes out clean. Remove from the oven and leave to cool in the pan.

While the cake is cooking, make the icing. Mix the coffee granules with a few drops of hot water to dissolve them. Melt the butter and brown sugar together in a small pan over a medium heat until the sugar dissolves. Then add the coffee to the pan. Leave to cool for a couple of minutes before sieving the icing sugar into the pan and mixing to combine.

When the cake is cooled, drizzle over the icing and serve.

Toffee apple cake

Toffee and apples are a match made in fruit heaven. A dreamy flavour combination that, for me, takes me back to fairgrounds and fireworks night. This cake celebrates those flavours and you could actually refer to it as a dessert. It is always best served warm with a generous dollop of the toffee sauce and vanilla ice cream, if you like.

Serves 12
Prep 20 mins
Cook 1 hour

For the cake
175 g (6 oz) unsalted butter,
   at room temperature
150 g (5 oz/⅔ cup) caster
   (superfine) sugar
200 g (7 oz/scant 1⅔ cups)
   self-raising flour
1 teaspoon ground cinnamon
½ teaspoon ground ginger
1 teaspoon baking powder
4 eggs, beaten
100 g (3½ oz/1 cup)
   ground almonds
50 g (2 oz/heaped ⅓ cup)
   sultanas (golden raisins)
200 g (7 oz) crisp eating
   (dessert) apples, such as
   Granny Smith or Chivers
   Delight, peeled, cored
   and sliced

For the toffee sauce
200 ml (7 fl oz/scant 1 cup)
   double (heavy) cream
50 g (2 oz) butter
175 g (6 oz/scant 1 cup) light
   muscovado sugar
1 tablespoon golden
   (light corn) syrup
1 tablespoon black
   treacle (molasses)

To serve
vanilla ice cream

Preheat a fan oven to 160°C (320°F/gas 4) and grease the base of a 23 cm (9 in) round springform cake pan with butter and line with baking parchment.

In an electric mixer, cream the butter and sugar together until pale and smooth. In a separate bowl, sift together the flour, cinnamon, ginger and baking powder.

Slowly add the beaten eggs to the butter mixture a little at a time, mixing well in between and introducing a tablespoon of the flour as you go. Once all the flour has been added, pour in the ground almonds and sultanas and mix until combined.

Add three-quarters of the apples to the mixture and stir in with a wooden spoon before spooning the cake mixture into the prepared pan. Arrange the final pieces of apple on the top of the cake in a circular pattern.

Bake in the oven for 1 hour until a skewer inserted in the middle comes out clean. Leave to cool in the pan for 5 minutes, then remove the springform ring and transfer to a wire rack to finish cooling.

To make the toffee sauce, put the cream in a saucepan over a low heat to warm. Add the butter and sugar and stir until dissolved and smooth. Then add the syrup and treacle and stir until melted.

Serve the cake with the hot toffee sauce and a hefty dollop of vanilla ice cream.

Danish apple cake (æblekage)

So simple to make but a stunning centrepiece for the table, this layered cake boasts
the complementary flavours and textures of apple and sponge, dusted with cinnamon.

Serves 8
Prep 10 mins + cooling
Cook 1 hour 10 mins

For the cake
225 g (8 oz/2 cups) caster
(superfine) sugar
225 g (8 oz) butter,
at room temperature
4 eggs, beaten
250 g (9 oz/2 cups) plain
(all-purpose) flour
1 teaspoon baking powder
½ teaspoon salt
1 teaspoon vanilla extract

For the apples
100 g (3½ oz/scant ½ cup)
caster (superfine) sugar
1 tablespoon ground cinnamon
500 g (1 lb 2 oz) crisp eating
(dessert) apples, such
as Granny Smith or Chivers
Delight, peeled, cored
and sliced

Preheat a fan oven to 180°C (350°F/gas 6) and grease a 23 cm (9 in) round
cake pan with butter and line with baking parchment.

In an electric mixer, cream together the sugar and butter until smooth.
Add the beaten eggs a little at a time, mixing well between additions.

Sift together the flour and baking powder and add a pinch of salt.
Gradually add to the mixer a spoonful at a time. Add the vanilla extract
and mix to combine.

In a separate bowl, mix together the sugar and cinnamon, then toss the
apples in to fully coat in the mixture.

Pour half of the cake mixture into the prepared cake pan. Layer about a third
of the apple slices on top and then pour over the rest of the cake mixture.

Finally, decorate the top of the cake with the rest of the apple slices,
creating a swirl or fan decoration with one slice overlapping the other
Sprinkle over any of the remaining cinnamon and sugar mixture.

Bake in the oven for 1 hour 10 minutes until a skewer inserted in the
middle comes out clean. You might find it needs more or less time in
the oven so keep a close eye on the cake, particularly towards the final
20 minutes to ensure it doesn't burn on top. If necessary, cover the cake
with foil for the very last part of baking.

Remove the cake from the oven and leave it to stand in the pan for
15 minutes until it is cool enough to handle, then remove the springform
ring and transfer to a wire rack to finish cooling.

Apple and cider brandy sorbet

The Somerset cider brandy or Calvados combined with the tartness of the apples makes this a refreshing after dinner pick-me-up. This is a slightly different way to make sorbet – a cheat's method if you will. You can easily make this recipe in an ice cream maker; however, if that is a luxury you aren't in possession of (and let's face it, who really needs all of those appliances taking up space in the kitchen) then this is a nice alternative route to making the popular, delicious frozen treat. I also generally find it easier and quicker to freeze the mixture in ice cube trays and blitz in a food processor. This method can result in a chunkier sorbet depending on the power of your machine, but I have never received any complaints.

Serves 4
Prep 15 mins
Freeze 4 hours

2 sharp, green eating
    (dessert) apples, such
    as Granny Smith, peeled,
    cored and chopped
juice of 1 lemon
100 g (3½ oz/scant ½ cup)
    caster (superfine) sugar
100 ml (3½ fl oz/scant
    ½ cup) water
2 tablespoons Somerset cider
    brandy or Calvados

Put the chopped apple, lemon juice, sugar and water into a food processor and purée for a couple minutes until as smooth as possible.

Next, pass the mix through a sieve (fine-mesh strainer) into a clean bowl to remove any lumps. Press the pulp through the sieve with the back of a spoon to get as much juice out as possible. Add the cider brandy and mix with a spoon.

Pour the mixture into ice cube trays and pop in the freezer for about 4 hours until completely frozen. You can also churn in an ice-cream maker if you have one. Just follow the manufacturer's instructions.

Take the cubes out of the freezer and whizz in the food processor once more to create a smooth sorbet. Refreeze for another 30 minutes and serve.

Raspberry and apple sorbet

A refreshing dessert or just a treat for a summer afternoon, the sweet raspberries contrast beautifully with the dash of fresh mint.

Serves 6
Prep 15 mins
Freezing 4 hours

300 ml (10 fl oz/1¼ cups)
  cloudy apple juice
50 g (2 oz/scant ¼ cup) caster
  (superfine) sugar
500 g (1 b 2 oz) fresh
  raspberries plus extra,
  to serve
small bunch of mint leaves,
  plus extra for garnish

In a saucepan, gently heat the apple juice and sugar until the sugar has dissolved into a syrup. Leave to cool to room temperature.

Meanwhile, place the raspberries and mint leaves into a food processor and blitz for a couple of minutes until completely smooth.

Pour the raspberry and mint juice through a sieve (fine-mesh strainer) into a clean bowl to remove seeds and any lumps.

Once the syrup has cooled, stir it into the raspberry and mint juice, then pour into ice cube trays and pop in the freezer for about 4 hours until completely frozen. You can also churn in an ice-cream maker if you have one. Just follow the manufacturer's instructions.

Just before you're ready to serve, take the cubes out of the freezer and whizz in the food processor once more to create a smooth sorbet. Refreeze for another 30 minutes. Then, serve with a few fresh mint leaves and raspberries to garnish.

Cider sorbet

A frozen, slightly alcoholic treat. Choose a strong, dry cider for maximum flavour in this refreshing sorbet.

Serves 4
Prep 20 mins
Freezing 4 hours

500 ml (17 fl oz/2 cups) water
400 g (14 oz/1¾ cups) caster
  (superfine) sugar
1 cinnamon stick
75 ml (2½ fl oz/
  5 tablespoons) lemon juice
250 ml (8½ fl oz/1 cup)
  dry cider

Heat the water, sugar and cinnamon stick in a pan over a medium heat until the sugar has completely dissolved into a syrup. Take off the heat to cool and remove the cinnamon stick.

Strain the lemon juice and mix with the cider. Combine with the cooled syrup, then pour into ice cube trays and pop in the freezer for about 4 hours until completely frozen. You can also churn in an ice-cream maker if you have one. Just follow the manufacturer's instructions.

When you're ready to serve, take the cubes out of the freezer and blitz in a food processor to create a smooth sorbet. Refreeze for another 30 minutes and serve.

Apple crumble ice cream

Apple crumble is so good, I thought I'd try it as an ice cream flavour too. This luxuriously creamy version combined with the crunchy crumble topping just hits the spot when you're in need of an ice cream fix. You may find that the apple results in it coming out of the freezer very hard, so take it out and let it stand for 10 minutes before scooping. All the better for building anticipation while you wait.

Serves 10
Prep 20 mins +
    overnight chilling
Cook 15 mins

For the ice cream
350 ml (12¼ fl oz/1½ cups)
    whole milk
300 ml (10 fl oz/1¼ cups)
    double (heavy) cream
1 vanilla pod (bean), sliced
    in half lengthways
6 egg yolks
150 g (5 oz/⅔ cup) golden
    caster (superfine) sugar

For the crumble
75 g (2½ oz/scant ⅔ cup)
    plain (all-purpose) flour
50 g (2 oz) butter
50 g (2 oz/½ cup) rolled oats
1 tablespoon demerara sugar
50 g (2 oz/½ cup) hazelnuts
    or walnuts, roughly chopped
a sprinkle of ground cinnamon

For the apples
30 g (1 oz) butter
50 g (2 oz/¼ cup)
    granulated sugar
500 g (1 lb 2 oz) cooking
    apples, such as Bramleys,
    peeled, cored and chopped

First make the ice cream. Put the milk, cream and vanilla pod in a saucepan over a medium heat and bring just to the boil.

Whisk the egg yolks in a bowl, then gradually add the caster sugar, whisking until smooth and pale. Gradually stir in the hot milk, whisking constantly. Transfer everything to the pan and, stirring constantly, gently heat until the mixture thickens like a custard. Remove from the heat and leave to cool. Cover the top of the ice cream with cling film (plastic wrap), to avoid a skin forming; and then chill in the refrigerator overnight.

Next day, make the crumble. Preheat a fan oven to 140°C (280°F/gas 3). Put the flour, butter, rolled oats and sugar in a bowl and rub between your fingertips until you get a breadcrumb-like texture. Add the nuts and a pinch of cinnamon and mix in well. Spread in a roasting pan.

Bake in the oven for 15 minutes until toasted and crunchy, stirring midway through to avoid it burning. Set aside to cool.

Prepare the apples by heating the butter and granulated sugar in a saucepan. Add the chopped apple and gently stew until the apple is cooked, but doesn't start to break down too much. You want nice firm chunks of stewed apple, not a sauce. You might need to add 1–2 tablespoons of water if it begins to stick. Set aside to cool completely before moving on to the next step.

Remove the mixture from the refrigerator and churn in an ice-cream maker until almost firm. Then gently fold in the apple mixture along with most of the crumble mix; leave some aside to serve. Churn gently until combined. Transfer to a freezer-proof container and freeze until ready to serve. Serve with a sprinkling of the crumble mix.

Homemade toffee apples

A fairground favourite and a recipe that will have children, big and small, come running, these are a special-occasion treat, of course, but a little bit of fun!

Makes 6
Prep 15 mins
Cook 10 mins

6 crisp eating (dessert)
  apples, such as Braeburn
400 g (14 oz/1¾ cups) golden
  caster (superfine) sugar
100 ml (3½ fl oz/scant
  ½ cup) water
1 teaspoon lemon juice
4 tablespoons golden
  (light corn) syrup

Fill a large bowl with boiling water, add the apples and leave for a minute or so. This removes any wax they may have on the skins and helps the caramel stick. Dry with paper towel and remove the stalks. Push a thick wooden skewer to about half way into each apple.

Line a baking sheet with baking parchment.

Put the sugar and water in a deep, heavy-based saucepan and bring to the boil. Reduce to a simmer until the sugar has dissolved, brushing any undissolved crystals down the side of the pan using a pastry brush. Add the lemon juice and syrup, stir carefully, then return to the boil. Heat the pan until the syrup reaches 150°C (300°F) on a sugar thermometer, or when a drop of the mixture forms a hard ball when dropped into cold water.

Have your prepared baking sheet next to the pan. One at a time, pick up each apple by the skewer and carefully turn it in the hot syrup mixture, coating the outside of the apple. Transfer the apples to the prepared baking sheet and leave to cool and harden.

Homemade toffee apples (176)

Drinks

Cider and apple juice are versatile drinks. While they stand up heartily on their own in the flavour stakes without any fuss, the sweet, fragrant and sometimes dry apple flavour complements and lifts many other drinks and ingredients too – from summer cocktails, spritzers and smoothies to festive winter mulled cider and apple tea, you'll find them all here.

Apple, carrot, beetroot and ginger juice

I like to think of the ingredients in this juice as the original superfood group. The flavours of the earthy beetroot with the sweetness of the carrots and sharpness of the apples and ginger make a delicious combination, a great hit of the detoxifying healthy fruits and veggies as well as an all-round tasty accompaniment to your breakfast or for any time of the day. You'll need a juicer for this recipe.

Serves 2
Prep 10 mins

2 whole beetroot
  (beets), quartered
3 carrots
2 sweet eating (dessert)
  apples, such as Golden
  Delicious or Greensleeves,
  cored and sliced
1 cm (½ in) piece of ginger root
ice cubes

Pass the vegetables, apples and ginger root through a juicer. Serve with some ice cubes.

Green apple juice

Anything this green must be really good for you, right? This smoothie makes a nice shot of green goodness when you're feeling in need of a little pick-me-up. You can even add a shot of wheatgrass powder for an added boost. You'll need a juicer and a blender handy to make this recipe.

Serves 2

Prep 5 mins

100 g (3½ oz) kale
100 g (3½ oz) spinach
2 crisp, tart eating (dessert)
   apples, such as Granny Smith
   or Cox's, cored and sliced
1 cm (½ in) piece of ginger root
½ cucumber, sliced
juice of ½ lemon
½ teaspoon runny honey
ice cubes

Pass all the fruit and vegetables through a juicer. Transfer to a blender and add the lemon juice and honey and a handful of ice and process on full power to mix.

Apple blossom infusion

Apple blossom is very fragrant and has citrus and rhubarb notes, so it makes a great infusion. You can actually just infuse it on its own in some hot water and it is delicious, but I like to add some dried apple and spices for a bolder-flavoured drink. You can find dried apple slices and apple blossom easily online but if you would rather, you can make this just using double the quantity of fresh apples, which have been cored and sliced.

Serves 4
Prep 5 mins
Cook 20 mins

100 g (3½ oz) dried apple slices
1 cinnamon stick
2 cloves
1 litre (34 fl oz/4 cups) water
10 g (¼ oz) dried apple blossom
about 1 tablespoon runny
    honey, to taste

Put the apple slices, cinnamon, cloves and water into a large saucepan over a medium heat and bring to the boil.

Reduce the heat to a very light simmer, add the apple blossom and heat for 15 minutes. Strain to remove the apple slices and spices and return the liquid to the pan.

Stir in some honey to taste and allow to dissolve. Serve hot.

Apple iced tea

Iced teas make for an idyllic and refreshing moment in the mid-afternoon heat. You can prepare this in a large batch overnight and then just help yourself as and when you need it throughout the day. Try using English Breakfast tea for this instead, if you prefer, but I like Earl Grey.

Serves 4
Prep 10 mins + steeping
   and overnight infusing
Cook 5 mins

1 litre (34 fl oz/4 cups) water
2 Earl Grey tea bags
1 cinnamon stick
1 litre (34 fl oz/4 cups) clear
   apple juice
2 tablespoons runny honey
1 lemon, sliced
2 crisp, sweet eating (dessert)
   apples, such as Cox's

To serve
ice cubes
sprig of mint or edible flowers

Bring the water to the boil in a saucepan, add the teabags and turn off the heat. Leave to steep for 20 minutes before removing the teabags.

Add the cinnamon stick, apple juice, honey and lemon slices and stir well to dissolve the honey. Leave to infuse overnight at room temperature.

When you're ready to serve, core and slice the apples and add them to the tea. Serve in glasses filled with ice cubes, then garnish with mint sprigs or edible flowers.

Uncle Mike's cider punch

Uncle Mike's Cider Punch is something that should carry a polite advisory note. While it is absolutely delicious and will have everybody coming back for more, it is certain to get the party started – no bad thing in my book.

My Uncle Mike used to serve this when the whole family got together at one of his many parties and autumn bonfires, and while we were never absolutely sure what he added into the punch bowl each time – and to be honest it was more a case of whatever he had spare would be thrown in, rather than a tried-and-tested recipe – he always created something that would give us rosy cheeks, warm hearts, and a rather quiet and subdued morning after. This is my dedication and my take on Uncle Mike's much-loved cider punch recipe.

Serves 4
Prep 10 mins

1 litre (34 fl oz/4 cups)
  medium dry cider
100 ml (3½ fl oz/scant
  ½ cup) dark rum
330 ml (11 fl oz/scant
  1½ cups) ginger beer
ice cubes
2 star anise
1 crisp, sweet eating (dessert)
  apple, such as Braeburn
  or Falstaff, cored and sliced
handful of strawberries and
  raspberries, halved
½ orange, sliced
soda water, to taste

Combine the cider, rum and ginger beer in a jug with plenty of ice. Add the star anise and fruit. Top up with soda water, to taste, and serve as a delicious long drink for lazy summer days.

Cider slushie

What happens when two of the most popular summer ingredients come together? Cider frosé, of course! The scrumptious combination of strawberry and apple flavours unites in the ultimate summer cool down. You can use leftover syrup as a drizzle over cakes or in other cocktails.

Serves 4
Prep 10 mins +
  overnight freezing
Cook 5 mins

750 ml (25 fl oz/3 cups)
  medium cider
100 g (3½ oz/scant ½ cup)
  caster (superfine) sugar
100 ml (3½ fl oz/scant
  ½ cup) water
200 g (7 oz) strawberries, hulled
4 tablespoons lemon juice
ice cubes

Pour the cider into an ice cube tray and freeze overnight.

Heat the sugar and water in a saucepan over a medium heat until the sugar has dissolved. Add the strawberries and cook for 2 minutes, then remove from the heat and leave to infuse for 45 minutes.

Strain into a clean bowl, ensuring you don't press down on the strawberries to squash them into the syrup too much. Leave the syrup to cool in the refrigerator until you're ready to serve.

To serve, take the cider cubes out of the freezer and place in a blender. Add the lemon juice, 100 ml (3½ fl oz/scant ½ cup) of the strawberry syrup and some ice and blitz until you have a smooth consistency. Enjoy!

Cider sangria

A not-so-traditional take on sangria, this apple version is a delicious, zesty and refreshing summer punch enjoyed especially on hot days with lots of ice. It's very easy to make and something completely different.

Serves 4
Prep 10 mins

2 crisp, green eating (dessert)
  apples, such as Golden
  Delicious, cored and sliced
1 orange, quartered and sliced
juice of ½ lemon
1 tablespoon runny honey
200 ml (7 fl oz/scant 1 cup)
  apple juice
3 tablespoons cider brandy
1 litre (34 fl oz/4 cups)
  sparkling dry cider
sprig of mint, stalks removed
ice cubes

Add the sliced apples, oranges, lemon juice and honey to a large punch bowl or jug and mix to dissolve the honey. Then add the other ingredients one by one and stir well to mix.

Winter cider Pimm's

A winter take on the traditional summer Pimm's punch, adding the spices and cider give the drink a distinctly Christmassy vibe. You can also warm this one up and make it into a mulled punch – simply omit the soda water and ice, and heat the other ingredients over a medium heat.

Serves 4
Prep 5 mins

250 ml (8½ fl oz/1 cup) Pimm's
500 ml (17 fl oz/2 cups)
  dry cider
250 ml (8½ fl oz/
  1 cup) soda water
1 cinnamon stick
½ juicy eating (dessert)
  apple, such as Egremont
  Russet, cored and sliced
½ orange, sliced
ice cubes

In a large jug, add the Pimm's, cider, soda water and cinnamon stick and stir. Add the apple, orange and a handful of ice cubes and stir once again, before decanting into glasses to serve.

Apple, ginger and chilli cocktail

Ginger and chilli with a hit of apple are warming autumn flavours that are sure to add some fire to your belly on cold nights. The heat of the chilli and ginger are complemented and soothed with the sweetness of the apple juice.

Serves 4
Prep 5 mins

120 ml (4 fl oz/½ cup) vodka
   or Apple vodka (page 210)
400 ml (13 fl oz/generous
   1½ cups) cloudy apple juice
800 ml (27 fl oz/scant
   3½ cups) ginger beer
ice cubes
1 crisp, red eating (dessert)
   apple, such as Fiesta
   or Honeycrisp, cored
   and sliced
small piece of ginger root,
   peeled and thinly sliced
½ bird's eye chilli, seeded
   and thinly sliced

Pour the vodka, apple juice and ginger beer into a jug and stir.

Add a few cubes of ice to four tumbler glasses along with some slices of apple, a slice of ginger root and a slice of chilli. Pour in the vodka mix and serve.

Cider Champagne cocktail

This is a West Country take on the traditional Champagne cocktail with cider brandy and apple, which provides something a little different in the flavour-wise compared to the usual recipe.

Serves 4
Prep 5 mins

4 sugar cubes
Angostura bitters, to taste
3 tablespoons Somerset
   cider brandy
1 bottle of Champagne
   or prosecco
½ sweet eating (dessert)
   apple, such as Pink Lady
   or Ambrosia, cored
   and sliced

Put a sugar cube in each of four Champagne glasses. Add a dash of bitters to each glass – you really don't need very much here, just enough for the sugar cube to absorb.

Add the cider brandy to the glasses and top up with the Champagne or prosecco. Garnish with a slice of apple, to serve.

Apple, rose and mint cocktail

This fragrant cocktail is delicate and aromatic as well as lightly refreshing. The flavours of apple, rose and mint make an interesting mix – just don't add too much rose water as it is very strong.

Serves 2

Prep 5 mins

100 ml (3½ fl oz/scant
   ½ cup) vodka
200 ml (7 fl oz/scant 1 cup)
   apple juice
2 drops of rose water
ice cubes
a few lemon balm leaves,
   plus extra to garnish
a few mint leaves or rose
   petals, to garnish
a few slices of apple,
   to garnish

Combine the vodka, apple juice and rose water in a cocktail shaker with ice. Add a few lemon balm leaves, reserving some for garnish, and shake well.

Pour the cocktail into 2 tumblers and garnish with a rose petal or mint leaf and a slice of apple.

Cider and thyme cocktail

Cider and apples bring a real zesty sweetness when paired with herbs in savoury dishes, which also works well in drinks. The fragrant, sunbaked aroma of thyme and the sweet dryness of the cider mixes well here to create something quite unusual.

Serves 2

Prep 10 mins

250 ml (8½ fl oz/1 cup)
  sparkling cider
50 ml (1¾ fl oz/
  4 tablespoons) vodka
squeeze of lemon juice
2 small sprigs of thyme
ice cubes
tonic water

Pour the cider into long glasses. Add the vodka and a squeeze of lemon juice. Add a stem of fresh thyme and leave to infuse for a minute or two.
  To finish, add ice and top up with tonic water.

Orchard cocktail

This is a new recipe that I have been trying out as a light summer drink. The flavours of apple and elderflower go famously well together, and the addition of cucumber gives the drink an extra burst of freshness, perfect for long summer days.

Serves 2

Prep 5 mins

100 ml (3½ fl oz/scant ½ cup) dry gin
150 ml (5 fl oz/scant ⅔ cup) apple juice
2 tablespoons elderflower cordial
ice cubes
¼ cucumber, sliced
½ apple, sliced
2–4 small sprigs of lavender

Pour the gin, apple juice and elderflower cordial into a cocktail shaker with some ice and muddle. Don't be too rough – you only need to combine.

Add the sliced cucumber and apple to two long cocktail glasses and pour over the gin mix.

Top with a lavender stalk or two, recline on the sun lounger and enjoy!

Somerset cider mule

A distinctly alternative take on the traditional Moscow Mule, this version adds cider to the mule's usual ginger beer and vodka flavours. A popular, zesty yet warming cocktail at dinner parties and get-togethers that packs a punch! If you don't have apple vodka, then add a splash of apple juice along with some regular vodka.

Serves 2
Prep 5 mins

100 ml (3½ fl oz/scant
   ½ cup) dry cider
100 ml (3½ fl oz/scant
   ½ cup) ginger beer
75 ml (2½ fl oz/
   5 tablespoons) Apple vodka
   (page 210), or regular vodka
   and a splash of apple juice
juice of ½ lime
crushed ice

Put the cider, ginger beer, vodka and lime juice in a cocktail shaker and lightly shake to mix.

Pour out into tumblers filled with crushed ice, to serve.

Cider sunrise

Easy to make and full of flavour, mixing apple and orange with cider and grenadine makes a punchy, but delicious pre-dinner drink served on the rocks.

Serves 2
Prep 5 mins

60 ml (2 fl oz/¼ cup)
   Apple vodka (page 210),
   or regular vodka and
   a splash of apple juice
3 tablespoons dry cider
100 ml (3½ fl oz/scant
   ½ cup) orange juice
ice cubes
1 tablespoon grenadine
apple peel, to garnish

Pour the vodka, cider and orange juice into a tall glass with a handful of ice.

Pour in the grenadine and serve with some twisted apple peel to garnish.

Apple and cinnamon martini

A Christmas or mid-winter take on the classic martini; apple and orange flavours from the vodka and Cointreau with the flavour of the cinnamon creates something slightly different from the norm.

Serves 2
Prep 5 mins

crushed ice
100 ml (3½ fl oz/scant
   ½ cup) Apple vodka
   (page 210), or regular vodka
   and a splash of apple juice
150 ml (5 fl oz/scant
   ⅔ cup) apple juice
1 teaspoon Cointreau
1 cinnamon stick
twists of apple peel,
   to garnish

Add some crushed ice to two martini glasses to chill.
   Put the apple vodka, apple juice, Cointreau and cinnamon stick in a cocktail shaker with some crushed ice. Shake for a minute to allow the cinnamon flavour to infuse.
   Discard the ice in the glasses and pour the cocktail out through a strainer to serve. Garnish with some twisted apple peel, to serve.

Honey and cider brandy sour

Cider brandy or Calvados and honey are bold yet soothing flavours. Adding the lemon juice and some soda water to top them up creates a drink that is packed with striking flavour.

Serves 2
Prep 5 minutes

100 ml (3½ fl oz/scant
   ½ cup) Somerset cider
   brandy or Calvados
2 teaspoons runny honey
3 tablespoons lemon juice
ice cubes
soda water
apple slices, to garnish

Put the cider, honey and lemon juice in a cocktail shaker filled with ice. Shake well for a minute or two so that the honey fully dissolves.
   Pour out through a cocktail strainer into two tumblers, top up with soda water and serve with a slice of apple as the garnish.

Somerset cider mule (204)

Apple and cinnamon martini (205)

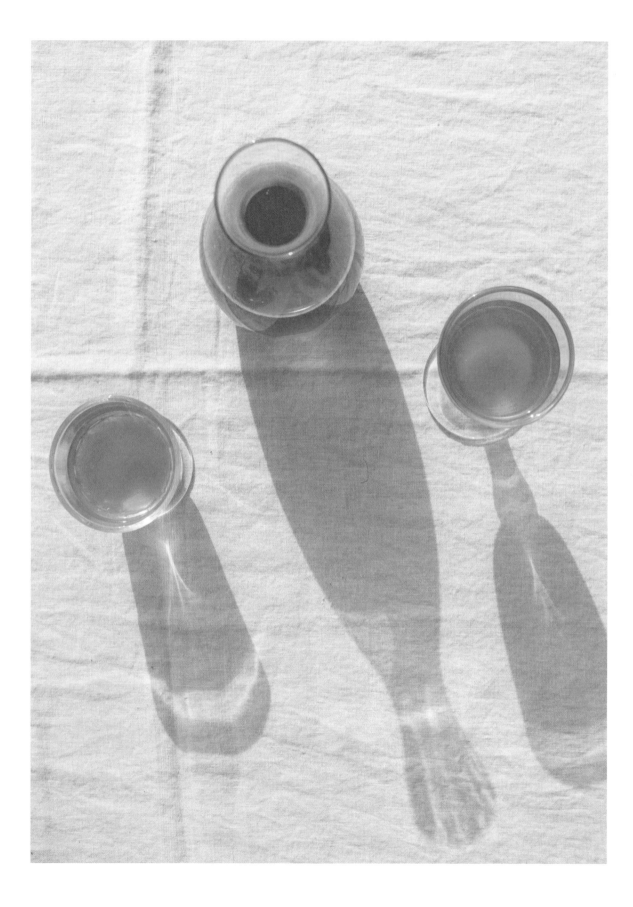

Apple cosmopolitan

This appley version of a traditional cosmopolitan uses my Apple vodka with elderflower cordial.

Serves 2
Prep 5 mins

crushed ice
50 ml (1¾ fl oz/
   4 tablespoons) Apple vodka
   (page 210), or regular vodka
   and a splash of apple juice
2 tablespoons lime juice
2 tablespoons triple sec
2 tablespoons elderflower
   cordial

Add some crushed ice to a martini glass to chill. Pour the apple vodka, lime juice, triple sec and elderflower cordial into a cocktail shaker along with a handful of the crushed ice and shake well.

Discard the ice in the martini glass and pour the apple cosmo out through a cocktail strainer.

Apple vodka

Infusing vodka with apple provides a great base for many a cocktail, and it can be even enjoyed on the rocks or with some elderflower cordial and sparkling water. The key here is to buy a plain vodka that isn't already flavoured with anything else – it needs to be clean tasting and good quality. You can also substitute some apples for blackberries or cinnamon and citrus for different takes on this infusion – just chop or slice them, there's no need to peel.

Makes 1 litre (34 fl oz/
   4 cups)
Prep 10 mins
Infuse 3–4 weeks

300 g (10½ oz) sharp, green
   eating (dessert) apples,
   such as Granny Smith's,
   Sturmer, Pipin or Cox's,
   cored and sliced
1 litre (34 fl oz/scant
   4 cups) vodka

Thoroughly clean a large Kilner (Mason) jar with a sealable lid. Add the apples to the jar.

Pour the vodka over the apples until they are fully covered. Seal the jar and leave it to stand to infuse in a cool, dry place for 3–4 weeks. Avoid anywhere that gets too warm.

As the vodka infuses it will take on the flavour of the apples and start to turn a light yellow colour that will darken the longer it is infused. Taste after a couple weeks to check the flavour and either continue or stop infusing according to preferred taste.

When the vodka has reached your ideal flavour, strain the apple pieces out and then pass the liquid through a muslin (cheesecloth) to remove any sediment.

Pour into individual bottles and label and seal until ready to drink.

Mulled apple juice with rhubarb and ginger

In this non-alcoholic version of the Traditional mulled cider (page 212), the rhubarb and ginger completely fill the room with an amazing spicy scent, and just one mug will be sure to warm you right through.

Serves 4
Prep 5 mins
Cook 6 mins

1 litre (34 fl oz/4 cups) cloudy
    apple juice
1 cinnamon stick
½ orange, sliced
¼ stick rhubarb
1 cm (½ in) piece
    of ginger root
2 teaspoons runny honey

Put the apple juice, cinnamon stick, orange slices, rhubarb and ginger root in a large saucepan and heat over a medium heat for 5 minutes. Don't let it boil. Sweeten with the honey and stir to dissolve for another minute.
    Ladle into heatproof glasses or mugs to serve.

Traditional mulled cider

This recipe reminds me of winter at home. As the cider warms, it completely fills the house and smells beautifully spicy, festive and heart-warming. It is the perfect concoction for an antidote to cold winter days. Growing up, my dad would make a pot of mulled cider in an old kettle and sit it on the wood burner to heat up and fill the room with this wonderfully comforting aroma. The result was something that resembled a rather heady, cider-infused steam-room. And some very jolly family members crowded round for a top up!

Serves 6–8
Prep 5 mins
Cook 10 mins

2 litres (70 fl oz/8 cups) traditional farmhouse scrumpy (Rich's Cider is best used here!)
4 cloves
1 star anise
1 cinnamon stick
1 orange, sliced
1 crisp sweet eating (dessert) apple, such as Cox's, cored and sliced
2 tablespoons runny honey, preferably Somerset

Pour the cider into a saucepan and add all the other ingredients. Heat over a medium heat until the cider is steaming but not boiling (this is very important as boiling cooks out the alcohol!).

Once warm, ladle into heatproof glasses or mugs and slurp the cold away.

Cider brandy hot toddy

The antidote to colds and flu that you won't find at the pharmacist, this hot toddy has a nice hit of brandy – or traditionally whisky – to help clear your head when you are feeling under the weather, along with the natural vitamin C kick from the honey and lemon juice.

Serves 2
Prep 5 mins

½ lemon
4 teaspoons runny honey
8 cloves
100 ml (3½ fl oz/scant ½ cup) Somerset cider brandy
2 apple slices
boiling water

Cut two slices from the lemon half. In two heatproof glasses with handles, or in two mugs, put the lemon slices, honey, cloves, a squeeze of lemon juice from the remaining lemon and cider brandy.

Add the slice of apple and top up the glasses with boiling water to serve.

I have learnt one massive life lesson while creating this book, and that is that things that push you outside of your comfort zone can be equally some of the scariest experiences of your life, but also some of the most rewarding and enriching too.

Writing *Apple* has been an incredible opportunity that has provided me with new and exciting experiences and challenges that I had never considered, or thought were possible. And for that I have some particularly supportive, creative and loving people to say thank you to.

Firstly, team Apple: Jacqui, Kathy, Wei, Evi, Emma, Eila, Rebecca and everyone else at Hardie Grant. Plus a very special thank you to Kate, who took a punt on a random guy from the sticks that I really hope has paid off! Your creativity and vision for this project has been an inspiration and I really hope you're as proud of this book as I am. Thank you to the many, many people who answered my desperate social media pleas for help testing the recipes; from neighbours and dear friends and colleagues to fellow foodies and complete strangers, each and every one of you were wonderfully supportive and this book is all the better for your help.

Alison, Rich, Jemma, Jamie, Ellie, Sarah and Emilie. Thank you for being so patient and understanding, and just generally putting up with me. Big love.

Rob, thank you for letting me cause havoc and mess up your kitchen during the shoots.

Jan, Brian, George and Molly and the rest of the team at Rich's Cider Farm. Thank you for all your support and time in helping us get the amazing pictures we were able to capture at the farm and in the orchards.

Dad, your knowledge and passion for your craft is an inspiration, and something that both I and the girls are very proud of. Thank you for all your help and for generally being awesome.

Thank you also to the rest of my family and friends for your love and support.

And finally, a little nod to the man that made me believe I could do it in the first place. You are the apple of my eye and thank you for your love and support throughout this process. *Apple* is as much yours as it is mine, as without you it simply wouldn't have happened. Pip, I do love you very much, you know.

About the Author

James Rich is a Somerset-born and bred, cider-maker's son. His family has been making a living from apples for centuries and what they don't know about the pomme, quite frankly, isn't worth knowing! James grew up helping his dad at work: planting the orchards, pressing the apples to gather the juice, and even helping to clean the giant 5,700-litre (10,000-pint) oak vats that are used during the fermenting process.

A passionate home cook, as a child James was encouraged to explore food and flavour in the kitchen by his grandmother, who showed him the basics and helped develop his cooking. Then, as a teenager, he worked in the cider farm's restaurant, which is where his love and passion for food continued to flourish. He now divides his time between Somerset and living in London, working as a food writer and brand consultant.

It was rediscovering some old family favourite recipes that gave James the idea for *Apple*, and a wealth of family knowledge gleaned from years watching the fruits grow and harvesting them in the orchard helped form the basis for a host of brand-new ideas, updating his heritage for a whole new generation of apple lovers.

Published in 2019 by Hardie Grant Books,
an imprint of Hardie Grant Publishing

Hardie Grant Books (London)
5th & 6th Floors
52–54 Southwark Street
London SE1 1UN

Hardie Grant Books (Melbourne)
Building 1, 658 Church Street
Richmond, Victoria 3121

hardiegrantbooks.com

British Library Cataloguing-in-Publication Data.
A catalogue record for this book is available from the
British Library.

Apple by James Rich
ISBN: 978-1-78488-232-7

Publishing Director: Kate Pollard
Junior Editor: Eila Purvis
Designers: Evi-O.Studio | Evi O & Susan Le
Copy Editor: Wendy Hobson
Proofreader: Jane Bamforth
Photographer: Jacqui Melville
Food Stylist: Kathy Kordalis
Prop Stylist: Wei Tang and Jacqui Melville
Indexer: Cathy Heath

Colour Reproduction by p2d
Printed and bound in China by Leo Paper Group